DO IT FOR YOU

How to Stop People-Pleasing and Find Peace

VANESSA OOMS

The Library and Archives of Canada catalogs the first edition of this book as follows:
Ooms, Vanessa
Do it for you: how to stop people-pleasing and find peace / Vanessa Ooms

ISBN 978-1-7387471-1-5 (ebook)
ISBN 978-1-7387471-2-2 (hardcover)
ISBN 978-1-7387471-0-8 (paperback)
ISBN 978-1-7387471-3-9 (audiobook)

Editorial Supervision: Michael Ireland
Cover and Interior Design: Vanessa Ooms

This book is dedicated to Ray and Kristen.

Thank you for always seeing the light within me.

Most of life is a play of energy.
Of transmuting all that could
drown you, into fuel to reach
heights one can only dream of.

– Suhaib Rumi

CONTENTS

•••

DO IT FOR YOU

PREFACE

The book you hold in your hands was created as a source of empowerment for whomever is meant to pick it up. Once I finished the early pages, this book wrote itself, waking me up in the night and calling to me to add to it at random times of the day. But we know how this universe works, don't we? There is nothing random about it. Every time I wrote a new chapter or section, a situation would crop up that beckoned me to embody the teaching even deeper. The process of bringing this book into the world was part magic and part practical application. My intention is that it will bring you a similar experience that will stretch you, embrace you, challenge you, and comfort you.

INTRODUCTION

*Sometimes life will tear your house apart so that you can
see the cracks in the foundation.*

In the twilight hours of a foggy day in 2015, I looked in the mirror and realized I didn't recognize myself anymore. It had been ages since I had gazed into my own eyes for any significant amount of time. "Who are you?" I asked my reflection as I investigated the new lines around my eyes, the faded color of my irises, and the exhausted spirit behind them. *What do I do now?*

The longer I stared at myself, the more emotions rumbled to the surface. Grief, deep sadness, and rage all bubbled up to meet me. Without breaking my gaze in the mirror, I watched tears pour down my face and felt a massive amount of energy move through my body.

I don't know how long I was in front of that mirror, but I realized I had a dull ache in my back and in the arches of my feet. I sat down. *Wow! Now what?* As I sat in the silence of the early morning hours, my body hollow, I examined my life, dissected the pathway that had led me to this moment. How did it all go so wrong? *How could I have thought I was on the right path, only to have everything blow up in my face? Is this a test from the universe?*

It was deeper than that. I knew in my heart of hearts that this moment was the culmination of choices I'd made that were not in my best interest; in which I had ignored my intuition and red flags, and done what I thought others would view as "right." I had no choice. I had to dive deep within. In one fell swoop I was living alone with my dog, with no vehicle,

15

a business I had to shut down (with all its related debts), no job, no trust in my fiancé or best friend... and worst of all... no faith. *How had I gotten so far off track? I was doing all the right things! How did I stray so far from my true self? From my....soul?*

I had buried and forgotten about my True Self long ago. If you watch my collection of old home movies, you will notice a point where a shift happened in me. I went from being a carefree, fun-loving little girl to a closed-off, overburdened, distrusting young woman. I grew up way too fast and was thrust into survival mode. The dreamer who had existed in my youth was a faded, distant memory, and so were her dreams. Somewhere along the line, I started doing what was practical, instead of what lit me up. The happiness and emotional well-being of the people in my circle became more important than my own. I worried more about what other people thought of me than what I thought of myself. I adopted the belief that the art that lived inside of me was wrong and that no one would want it... or me.

I lost myself. My True Self—the one who lives behind the masks, the expectations, the doing, and the order. The one who is divine in nature and powerful beyond measure. The one made of love. I fell into the rabbit hole of people-pleasing and hit rock bottom with a sickening smack. And now everything was still... and dark... and excruciatingly quiet.

I had been moving so quickly through life there wasn't time for self-reflection. Most of my life, I had been running. I thought I was running toward achievement and success, but I was running from my True Self, whom I had shut away in a tiny closet inside my subconscious mind. That self had been screaming, banging on the door day-in and day-out for decades. The only way I could drown out the noise of my spirit was to run through life so quickly that the sound of chaos and time whizzing by me was louder than the call of my soul. There was nowhere to run now. All I could do was sit in this dark, empty, quiet pit of nothingness and ponder every choice I had made. Sit in this emptied-out body and listen to that still small voice I had been ignoring. Sit and get reacquainted with myself... my soul... my truth.

Thus began the years-long unraveling of the false self and life I'd constructed, and the deconstruction of decades of conditioning and limiting beliefs. Every piece I chiseled off the mask of my false self revealed more of the light of my spirit. Every time I discovered more of my inner light, my body and mind went through an acclimation process. Sometimes that process was delicious, other times it was uncomfortable stretching. But every time I healed and integrated more of the hurting parts of myself, I became more grounded, strong, confident, unshakeable. Every time I faced an aspect of myself I had deemed undesirable and offered it love, I realized I could be my own best friend. I didn't need validation from outside myself. Every time I stood up for myself and established boundaries, it reaffirmed that the opinions and projections of others were not my cross to bear. Each time I made decisions that served me, rather than trying to please others, I felt safer within my body. I realized that if no one else had my back throughout life, it was okay, because I was here for myself now.

*

Over years of deep work, prayer, and surrender, I unshackled myself from the emotions and projections of others, the harsh expectations I had of myself, and the conditioning of a society that does not value the empowerment of its people. Coming home to my True Self, coming to know God, surrendering to deep soul healing and reclaiming my personal power has been transformative. My reality and experience of life has shifted into unconditional love, true abundance, freedom, and creative fire.

I want to share what I've learned along this journey, hoping I can help others on the path of rediscovering themselves. This is the book I wish I'd found while I was going through this unraveling. I hope it serves you in coming home to your True Self.

Before we dive into the details of this book, I invite you to pick a spot that will be your safe space as you do this work. I have an armchair I can sink into, put on my headphones, and drift into my world. My other safe spaces are the garden and the bathtub. Have somewhere you can go to process everything that comes up.

Much love,
V

P.S. This is not just another book you can blaze through and chuck on the bookshelf. It is an *interactive manual* that can help you create real, lasting change in your life. There is a lot of information available in the world today, but it is what we choose to *do* with this information that dictates how our lives turn out. Only your practical application of these concepts will generate a life-changing experience. For this reason, I've compiled a collection of supplemental material to help you along your journey through this book. Those include:

• Guided meditation videos

• Do It For You Book Club — an online gathering where we come together to go through the content of this book and share our experiences along the way

• A downloadable list of affirmations you can print out and tape to your mirror

• Printable journaling prompts for self-discovery on many different topics

Links to these resources can be found at the end of this book. If you'd like to contact me, you can reach me at <u>vanessa@vanessaooms.com</u>. I promise to read every message. If it takes a while to receive a response, please know that I'm getting through my correspondence as quickly as I can and you *will* receive a note back. You've got this.

CHAPTER 1

What is People-Pleasing?

*Belonging is the innate human desire to be part of some-
thing larger than us. Because this yearning is so primal,
we often try to acquire it by fitting in and by seeking
approval... true belonging only happens when we present
our authentic, imperfect selves to the world...*[1]

—Brené Brown, *Braving the Wilderness*

The desire to make others happy and have them regard you in a positive light is natural. We are social beings. We desire connection and
want to interact positively with someone and deepen that connection.
Those who fall into the trap of people-pleasing are attuned to the needs
of the people around them. During their development, people-pleasers
decide that the needs of everyone around them are more important and
pressing than their own. This can cause great tension in relationships
(and in the body), leading the people-pleaser to feel exhausted, dissatis-
fied, and resentful.

I have used silliness and defiance to mask my hurt feelings. I would
laugh things off or make it known that I was not bothered, so no one could
see my mushy spots and poke at them. I convinced myself I was protecting myself by doing this. I couldn't let the other person "win" or see my
weakness. I also made a story for myself that by not saying anything, I
was practicing non-attachment and being the bigger person. Meanwhile,

---

[1] Brené Brown, *Braving the Wilderness* (New York: Random House, 2019).

I would *fume* inside for days, weeks, or even months, not knowing how to move the emotion through my body and process it. What I didn't realize was that by doing this, I was suppressing my emotions (anger) and denying my reality. This was another layer of people-pleasing, I realized, because I didn't want to make the other person uncomfortable by confronting them. So, I stuffed everything down, and then exploded when I got prodded one too many times. I'm not proud of this, but it was the way I knew how to operate in the world. I had never seen or known anything different. It felt like an invisible prison cell. Every nerve in my body was fried. I suffered with anxiety, depression, and panic attacks. I felt out of control, like I was at the mercy of everyone who came into my sphere. It took me years to realize I was giving my power away to everyone around me, debilitating myself. I was a leaf in the wind, being blown about by the gusts of other people's words, actions, emotions, and energies. I felt helpless, hopeless, and alone…and did not know how to change it!

But how do you know if you're a people-pleaser and not just burnt out? If any of the following statements resonate for you, you are most likely a people-pleaser:

TEN SIGNS YOU'RE A PEOPLE-PLEASER

1. You struggle with low self-esteem.

2. You have a hard time saying "No," to people.

3. If you do say "No," you often feel guilty.

4. You are preoccupied with what people are thinking about you.

5. You worry that turning people down will make you appear mean, lazy, or selfish.

6. You agree to things you don't like, don't agree with, or don't want to do so you don't rock the boat.

7. You want people to like you and feel that doing things for them will earn their approval.

8. You never have free time because you are always doing things for other people.

9. You apologize A LOT.

10. You don't admit when your feelings are hurt.

Sound familiar?

I know it might make you cringe to admit these things, but it is the first step to making real, lasting changes in your life. If you identify with the above statements and think you are a people-pleaser, high-five for you! This means you've got a good heart and you want to do good things in the world. People-pleasers are empathetic, caring, and thoughtful. That is nothing to be ashamed of.

However, where this can get toxic for you is when:
- The needs of others override your own.
- You have less and less time for yourself, your loved ones, and the things that are important to you because your time is already spoken for.
- You feel exhausted all the time because you have zero time to recharge
- You feel resentful every time someone asks you to do something.
- You daydream about ways that you can just check out and escape your life.

THE FOUR FEARS THAT CREATE PEOPLE-PLEASERS

Fear is like a 60-foot, two headed snake as big around as
a Ponderosa Pine. Avoid it and the snake grows larger
and comes closer, rearing its ugly head, ready to strike.
But look the snake in the eye, and it sees its own reflec-
tion, gets scared and shrinks away.

—Southwestern Native American Myth

It never occurred to me that I had the choice to say "No" to the demands of others. My mission in life was to make sure that everyone around me was okay. Once I entered my early teenage years, feeling lost, drained, and empty became my normal, and I didn't find anyone I could talk to about it. So, I became an expert at hiding the existential dread I felt, and everyone thought I was a happy-go-lucky girl who got along with everyone.

21

If only they had known. Living with this gaping hole in my soul while plastering a smile on my face was lonely. It lasted for years, until I got a massive slap-in-the-face wake-up call when my fiancé slept with my best friend. I had to examine my life.

As I explored the minutiae of the path that had led to destruction, I realized I hadn't become a people-pleaser because I wanted to be nice and help other people. I had given control of my life over to others out of fear. Fear had taken over my life and stolen my peace. I believed that if I acted in certain ways, I'd avoid situations I feared. However, the complete opposite happened. I ended up having to face all these fears, anyway. I believe the following fears are the reason so many of us become people-pleasers. Do any of these resonate for you?

1. Fear of rejection or abandonment

One of the core fears human beings share is the fear of rejection or abandonment. We all express this fear in different ways and filter the fear through different lenses, but it lives within all of us. We are wired for connection and want to avoid criticism. When you bump up against a situation that triggers this fear, you feel it in your bone marrow. It feels like a threat to your survival. On a deeper level, it threatens your essence and identity. But what is it we're really afraid of?

On a cognitive level, we may be afraid that rejection will confirm our worst fear—that we're unlovable, have little value or worth, or will be alone forever. These thoughts can make us agitated and anxious, and if they spin in our mind, we can spiral into the depths of existential crisis. Cognitive-based therapies can help us identify these disastrous thoughts and replace them with healthier thought patterns. Chapter 9 shares ways you can create a healthier environment for yourself inside your mind.

We may fear rejection because we are averse to pain and unpleasant experiences. Being human, we long to be accepted and wanted. It hurts to be rejected or experience loss, so we avoid this hurt in a multitude of ways—some obvious, some subtle. Rejection avoidance comes in many forms:

- Trying to please everyone—hence this book!

- Withdrawing and not asking for help

- Not expressing our true feelings

- Cutting people off at the first sign of conflict before they can reject us

- Avoiding new opportunities

- Putting on a disingenuous public persona that hides "the real you"

- Not speaking up

- Behaving in a passive/aggressive way to avoid facing rejection head-on

While these behaviors may help you avoid the short-term pain of rejection, they can lead to long-term problems in your relationships and a sense of loneliness. For tips on how to stop caring what people think of you, visit Chapter 7.

2. Fear of conflict or anger

Conflict avoidance is a people-pleasing behavior that arises out of a fear of upsetting others. The tendency to avoid conflict can be traced to growing up in an environment that was dismissive, hypercritical, or explosive. People who deal with conflict in this way walk on eggshells—expecting negative outcomes and having a hard time trusting the other person's reactions. In this situation, even voicing your opinion can become unnerving. Though it might seem like avoiding conflict and being the "nice one" is the best course of action, in the end, you are hurting yourself and your relationships. When you dismiss your legitimate feelings in favor of being "nice," you store frustration in your body, which can lead to a variety of health issues. A study conducted in 2013 found that bottling up your emotions can lead to an increased risk of premature death[2] and death from cancer. Yikes....

Not only does avoiding conflict affect your physical health, it can affect your mental and emotional health and your intimacy with others. When you suppress your true feelings to avoid conflict, you cut off honest

[2] Benjamin P. Chapman et al. "Emotion Suppression and Mortality Risk Over a 12-Year Follow-Up," Journal of Psychosomatic Research, Volume 75, Issue 4 (2013): 381-385, ISSN 0022-3999.

communication with others. This can lead to loneliness and depression—feeling like there is no one in the world who understands you. But how can anyone understand the true you when they are never allowed to see it? In Chapter 8, we go over ways to say "No," set boundaries and deal with conflict in a productive, healthy manner.

3. Fear of criticism or being disliked

Nobody enjoys being criticized or disliked, particularly people-pleasers. We hold other people's good opinions of us in high regard, and think that accommodating everyone else will shelter us from criticism. That's rarely the case. If you don't voice your concerns and speak your truth, people will assume you're happy to go along with whatever they want. They'll also assume that you'll accept disrespectful behavior. People-pleasers then become an easy target for other people's dissatisfaction and nastiness. When we overestimate the importance of the opinions of others in this way, we hand our personal power over to them. Dreading other people's negative opinions makes you feel trapped—like you can't show your fallible, authentic self. You hide behind a mask of niceness, and have a hard time separating your self-worth from your actions. Because you place importance on other people's opinions and spend time and energy trying to win them over, criticism can feel overwhelming. In Chapter 7, we go over ways you can stop caring so much about what other people think of you and set yourself free.

4. Fear of losing control or not being needed

People-pleasers *need to be needed*, believing it's their responsibility to make everyone around them feel better. Because our self-worth is tied to other people's happiness, when we make them feel better, we feel in control and like we're needed. On the flip side, if we cannot make someone feel better, we feel we've let them down. For myself, I'd become anxious if I couldn't soothe someone or help them. I'd absorb their negative energy, making it my responsibility to deal with it. Little did I know I was trying to control their emotional state so *I could feel better*.

But this isn't our responsibility. We're not meant to carry the emotional burden of the people around us. Nor are we meant to overstep to fix everything for everyone. It's an exercise in futility that leaves us feeling burnt out and taxed. The sky won't fall if you can't help someone. You don't have to rush in and save the day, losing yourself in someone else's business. You can only control your side of relationships. Once this knowledge sinks in, you can release your hold on the emotions of others and hold space for others while staying grounded in your own energy.

In Chapter 3, we explore the dynamics of codependency, and throughout the book we'll discuss a multitude of healthy ways we can relate to each other.

THE UNDERLYING CAUSES OF PEOPLE-PLEASING

In order to stop being a people-pleaser, you need to understand the underlying causes of the habit.

- **Poor Self-Esteem:** Because of a lack of self-confidence, people-pleasers seek external validation and think that doing things for others will win their approval.

- **The Need to Please:** People-pleasers agree to things they don't agree with or say "Yes" to things they don't want to do because they are concerned about what the other person will think of them if they don't. The need to please stems from a need to control outcomes and other people's opinions.

- **Perfectionism:** Wanting to make everyone around you happy stems from the need to have everything be perfect, from your performance to how others think and feel... all of which boils down to *control*.

- **Painful Experiences**: Painful or traumatic experiences can cause one to slip into people-pleasing behavior. Abuse survivors, for example, may default to being agreeable and pleasing others to avoid triggering others' abusive behavior. One might also turn to people-pleasing to avoid being reprimanded at work, which compounds poor self-esteem and triggers a perfectionist response.

The good news is there are solutions to break free of the *habit* of people-pleasing and to live a life of balance, fulfillment, and peace. That's what I plan to show you in this book.

Let's Break It Down:

I am sharing everything here with the intention that it will be used as a tool for *expanding your awareness and empowering you.* Having people-pleasing tendencies is not a reason to beat yourself up—and it is not a life sentence. I want you to see this behavior for what it is, so you can become aware of when you slip into people-pleasing patterns, and *choose something different in the moment.* This book is about taking responsibility for yourself; building a better life for yourself. *You* are the only one who can do that. The good news is that you are more than capable of doing this for yourself!

CHAPTER 2

My Journey with People-Pleasing

I put on the mask and robe, thinking that it would help me fit in. But soon the plaster crumbled and the fabric frayed, showing my true skin.

I grew up in an idyllic mining town called Elkford, which is nestled in the Rocky Mountains of British Columbia, Canada, along the Elk River. The name Elkford is derived from the Elk River, and the name of the original coal mining company the town was built on—Fording Coal. With a few thousand residents making up the town's population, there was a strong community vibe, everyone knew everyone, and as kids, we felt safe to go anywhere unattended. We spent tons of time outdoors. Wildlife was abundant all around us and it wasn't unusual to see moose, cougar, lynx, black bear, deer, or big-horned sheep around town and in the surrounding mountains. We even had a little ski hill with nine runs right in town. Many families were ski enthusiasts—as were the teachers and kids in my school.

Unlike a lot of kids, I enjoyed school. I've always loved learning new things and you could find me most often with my nose in a novel, a non-fiction book, or a sketchbook. Early on, I realized I was sensitive and compassionate. I felt everything deeply and could never wrap my mind around the violence in the world. I couldn't understand the way people treated each other "out there." My parents saw how sensitive I was and tried to shelter me from the harsh realities of the real world, but when

I was about eleven, they got divorced. I got a crash course in how life operates.

Growing up, I never saw my parents argue. They never raised their voices to each other and never got violent. But there was a tension in the house that was palpable. The only time I really witnessed conflict and arguments between them was when they went separate ways. I realized later in life that this experience cemented for me the belief that any conflict meant the imminent end of a relationship, and this fear of conflict and abandonment was what fueled my people-pleasing and codependent behavior.

I remember trying to do whatever I could to make my parents happy and to make their divorce go smoothly. I'm not sure why I took this upon myself…perhaps to deal with my own emotions? But I assumed the role of Mediator, and this title followed me through my young adult life. Whenever there was conflict around me, I tried to fix it. I saw both sides of any argument and tried to explain to either side what the other needed. When someone was upset around me, I'd listen to them, let them cry on my shoulder, and offer solace or advice. I wanted to smooth the waters— conflict made me jittery. When I could calm things around me down, I could calm myself. When I wasn't able to "do my job," I retreated into the forest alone and sat at the base of my favorite tree, where it was quiet and there were no expectations. I can't remember exactly when my step-parents entered my life, but what I do recall is the *tension and arguments*.

Melding families was not easy, and it taxed me. There seemed to be fighting between the camps all the time. I passed notes back and forth and felt like I was in the middle of conflict more often than not. There were certain people in the family dynamic I could not get along with, no matter how hard I tried. And I did try…to empathize, to sympathize, to listen, to bargain, to mediate, to compromise, and to appease…all to no avail. With these people, I was constantly walking on eggshells, never able to gauge their reactions, never knowing what was coming next. I tried so hard to appease these people that it didn't even occur to me that I was enduring abusive behavior. I was so anxious, I joined as many extracurricular activities as I could, so I could spend as little time at home as possible. It took twenty years of trying to realize I would never have an authentic or healthy relationship with these people.

Dancing was one of my places of solace during this time of familial transition. I could be present and tune the rest of the world out when I was dancing. It allowed me to express the emotions percolating inside my body and gave me an outlet to show my true face. But after my parents' divorce, there wasn't room in the budget for my lessons. So, I approached my teacher—could I work for her to pay for my lessons? She had me teach her group of five- and six-year-old kids to tap dance, and this brought me so much joy! They all called me "Ms. Vanessa" and couldn't wait to make noise with their tiny feet. It was beyond adorable and brought light to my life when I needed it.

As much as I loved Elkford for all its natural beauty and strong community, I couldn't *wait* to get out of there and move out on my own. Independence became my salvation. I got the first driver's test appointment on the morning of my birthday—on my fourteenth birthday for my Learner's License and on my sixteenth birthday for my full license. My bags were packed before my high school graduation ceremony was over.

As I ventured out into the world, the chronic anxiety I felt in childhood never left me. In all of my relationships—romantic, friendship, or business—I played the role of Mediator and Problem Solver for everyone. Always wanting to be perceived as "nice," I got into precarious situations—and some dangerous ones! I let people take advantage of me, disrespect me, even do me harm, all because I had a hard time saying "No" to anyone. I was so afraid of upsetting people, I avoided it at all costs.

Though I appeared confident, I had extreme social anxiety. I gauged how others were feeling around me, scoped out their reactions to everything I said and did. What pleased them? Where shouldn't I tread? I got a reputation for being amiable because I could be a chameleon and fit myself into any situation. I could be a mechanic, a barista, an academic, a hippy, an artist, a party girl, you name it! With a semi-photographic memory, I picked things up quickly (including other people's preferences), and could mold myself into a version of me they would accept. But I never felt a strong sense of identity, and this emptiness followed me wherever I went.

I never wanted to burden anyone with my problems—I thought they had enough of their own. I suffered in silence for years, dealing with anxiety, depression, and panic attacks. I became addicted to alcohol and work (for the numbing they offered), and I daydreamed of escaping to an island where I could be anonymous. I had suicidal thoughts. All of this while putting a smile on my face and being a "happy helper." Getting lost in helping others took my mind off the loneliness I felt, even when I was surrounded by people. Had I been dropped off on the wrong planet? Had someone *up there* made a mistake?

"I'm fine" became my mantra—an easy way to avoid expressing my genuine emotions or having a breakdown if someone asked me "How are you doing?" During my 20s, I was overextended, exhausted, unfulfilled. That decade feels like a blur. I was moving so quickly, giving a wide berth to the reality of a traumatic sexual assault I'd endured when I was in my late teens. To this day I only remember bits and pieces of that day, and there is still a huge chunk of time after this happened that I cannot locate in my memory. I guess I blocked it out. I felt so ashamed that I never told anyone about it. I just stuffed it down and started running through life. I became a high functioning alcoholic, drinking every day to numb the shame, depression and rage that I carried. All the while, I built self-worth through outward accomplishments—which included making others around me happy and overachieving in school and work. I graduated college and design school with honors, got promoted anywhere I worked, managed multiple businesses while also freelancing. My Type A perfectionism allowed me to hide the fact that I was dealing with dark emotions and thoughts daily. At night they'd all rush in to meet me, and I'd need to numb again. No one knew that I had any issues because I was so good at enacting my superhero persona and I made it my mission to create a calm oasis for anyone I interacted with. I wanted others to feel seen and heard and safe, all the things I wanted to feel myself but couldn't.

I'd lost touch with my intuition and fell into a perpetual "Yes" cycle, agreeing to everything requested of me without question—or even contemplation. One of my bosses called me "The Okay Lady," because I said "okay" to *everything*. *All the time.* Someone can't make their shift today? Okay, I can do a double shift. You can't make rent this month? Okay, I'll give you money and not pay my rent. You need help moving? Okay, I'll be there tomorrow.

I had lost control of my life, yet my pride kept me in this vicious cycle. I felt like if I turned someone down, they'd perceive me as lazy or selfish, and *I could not have that.* I felt vulnerable, like I might crack at any moment. I was walking a worn-out tightrope over a pit of despair. My nervous system was shot. I didn't know how to make it stop or how to feel better. I assumed this was going to be my reality forever... until I got body slammed by the universe.

In a short span of time, two of my family members passed away, I was betrayed by my fiancé and best friend, I closed the business I had run with my fiancé, had to find a vehicle ASAP, and I lost a bunch of friends. I got sick, discovered black mold in my house, and ended up working three jobs to make ends meet. There were many days where I didn't have enough money to feed myself. And those were just the big events. That year, everything that could go wrong did. I was broken. I didn't know who I was. And because I didn't want to burden anyone with what I was going through, I isolated myself from everyone who could have helped me. I didn't trust anyone, not even myself. When my fiancé and best friend admitted that they'd been sleeping together (for how long no one knows–they both told me different stories) and asked me to keep their secret in our small community, I did. That was when I realized that something was seriously wrong with the way I was living.

> *Someone I loved once gave me a box full of darkness.*
> *It took me years to understand that, this too, was a gift.*[3]
>
> —Mary Oliver

There's a unique type of fracturing that happens inside your spirit when you pour your being into someone, only to have them betray you. It's hard to put into words the visceral sensation that follows a heart injury like this... it seeps through the skin, muscle, and bone to the marrow and blood, and rips you apart from the inside out. It unravels your persona and perception. The foundation beneath you crumbles. In the topsy turvy trials that follow, you can't discern which way is up and which truth is true. Was the love a facade? Did my intuition lead me astray? Did I even matter? Did any of it matter?

I sat on my kitchen floor weeping for hours. I couldn't shut the floodgates. Every time breath heaved out of my lungs, the rawness of my spirit

---

[3] Mary Oliver, "The Uses of Sorrow," from *Thirst* (Boston: Beacon Press, 2007).

was accentuated. The core of my soul was screaming in agony. Writhing in pain, I wondered, *Will I survive this? Is it worth surviving this?* As darkness enveloped my home and my being, the experience confirmed my deep-seated belief: *I am not good enough.* This belief had been with me for as long as I could remember, manifesting in a multitude of ways I hadn't perceived until that moment. *Wow.* Puzzle pieces from my past floated through my mind, showing me that I had been manifesting situations to confirm my not-enough-ness. *I had been betraying myself.*

I don't know how long I wailed...but then came overwhelming, excruciating yet comforting... quiet. I didn't know this kind of sound vacuum was possible. I heard nothing—no birds outside, no appliances whirring, no phone notifications, no thoughts, no breath. Nothing. It was as if God had placed a glass jar over me the way I would over a rescued spider, and removed anything that would take me out of this presence. There was a small, quiet part of me who wanted to speak. As I waited, a long-lost piece of my soul emerged.

I did not speak for what seemed like days. I pieced together what was true for me and what was not. I saw which parts of my personality were authentic and which were formed out of fear. I saw how I had put the wellbeing and comfort of everyone in my life ahead of my own; how I had taken pride in that. *So selfless,* I told myself. But I had forgotten about and disregarded myself. It was not balanced. I had not been balanced. The tightrope I had been walking had just snapped. This led me to the moment I described in the Introduction to this book—I had to rebuild my life from scratch. I couldn't keep living the way I had been living. It was inauthentic, shallow, and unfulfilling for my soul. If I was going to live the life I wanted to live, I was going to give my *entire life* an overhaul.

This was no small feat. I made a *lot* of missteps along the way. I hurt some people's feelings with my stumbling. There were a lot of things I could have done better. But, as I worked with mentors, faced my demons, deepened my spiritual life, and grew into my authentic presence and voice, the need to people-please started to dissipate. I realized that people-pleasing was a mechanism used to fuel my false self, and that false self was fading away. I started sleeping better at night and experienced fewer panic attacks. Depression reared its head less and less. I saw life with a whole new perspective.

The first step in this process was admitting I had a problem. I had to acknowledge all the areas in my life where I had porous or no boundaries (which turned out to be pretty much every area of my life!), recognize where I was giving my power away, and see how I had co-created these situations in which I was overextending myself. Yeesh.

As I created personal boundaries and enforced them, I got to see who had my best interests at heart and who was benefiting from me being a pushover. Showing up for myself in this way created a new sense of confidence. I took care of myself in the same way I'd looked after the people around me. This was true self-love.

Full disclosure… it took the greater part of seven years to get to where I'm able to write this book. I hope that by implementing the material in these pages, you will get off the people-pleasing hamster wheel in a fraction of that time. If you approach the material and exercises in this book with an open mind and willing heart, you will achieve great transformation.

You've got this!

CHAPTER 3

Approval Addiction & Codependency

You are not required to set yourself on fire to keep other people warm.

—Unknown

At a young age, I adopted the belief that there was something wrong with me and that I needed to work for love—to prove my worth. I thought that in order to *be liked* by the people around me, I needed to *be like* them. So, I learned to study others and figure out what their preferences were so I could mirror them. It never occurred to me that I should like myself. I was so focused on external things, my inner world got little attention. I'd have moments of joy, but would slip back down into a chasm of sadness, longing for a home I wasn't sure existed. My notebooks were filled with little figures I drew with holes through the middle of them. Later in life, I saw that in those drawings, I was expressing how I felt.

Around grade 8, I learned I could keep existential dread at bay by being busy all the time, keeping my mind and hands working. I enrolled in every extracurricular activity I could. I joined student council, the yearbook committee, the designated driving club, soccer, dance, you name it. Most of my time outside of school hours was spoken for. I came home, ate dinner, did my homework, read a bit of a book, and passed out.

If you had told me all those years ago I was addicted to approval and seeking validation, I would have laughed. I had built a firm story in my head—I was independent and strong... the diplomatic peacekeeper, the fixer. I didn't realize I'd become these things so I could hide how vulnerable I felt. I wanted to be a hero, and to avoid conflict at all costs. Conflict to me meant the end of the world.

As I moved through adolescent life into adulthood, I approached all of my relationships with diligence, tip-toeing around the underlying fear that conflict could mean the end of the relationship. This approach got me into toxic, sometimes abusive, situations. I was so focused on keeping the peace and making sure that the other person approved of me, I ignored red flags. I waved off intuitive warnings, believing I was being "too judgmental." Unbeknownst to me, my "being nice" created an entryway for chaos and unhealthy relationships.

Since you're reading this book, it's safe to assume you believe yourself to be a "nice" person. I've got a couple of questions for you:

- Do you believe you are also a "kind" person?
- Do you believe "nice" and "kind" are the same thing?

I ask because I see well-intentioned, compassionate, empathetic people tripping themselves up. As I healed from my people-pleasing compulsion, I had to learn the difference between these terms. "Nice" (for most of us) is part of our *social conditioning*. Being "kind" means that you will sometimes not be perceived as nice.

Like most North American women, I was taught to be "good" and "nice," which are just cute labels for being quiet and passive. When I voiced my feelings, I was told I was "too sensitive." Over time, I internalized this voice. I told myself I *was* too sensitive; that there was something wrong with me. This toxic cycle of suppressing my emotions and gaslighting myself continued until I hit my breaking point. It was wild to see how ingrained this conditioning was—I'm working on reprogramming my mind to this day.

APPROVAL ADDICTION

We all want intimacy... and I'm not talking about sex. Real intimacy is when you can show all of yourself to someone—the good, the bad, and the ugly—and be loved for it all. True intimacy comes from vulnerability, and vulnerability comes from authenticity. Vulnerability is scary, though, so we try to get the approval, unconditional love, and intimacy we desire through showing others our *good side*. While this sounds like it might work, what we're doing is showing *ourselves* a *conditional* type of love. We're saying to ourselves, "I will only love these parts of you; therefore other people will only love these parts of you." We think that if we show our most desirable traits and get someone to like us first, then we can show them the rest later and they'll be cool with it. Often, though, the opposite happens. Then we wonder why we can't make relationships work!

It's common for folks to relate in this way, because so many of us grew up in an environment in which others showed us that parts of our expression are acceptable, while others are not. When we are mirrored in this way growing up, we lose our sense of self and begin searching outside ourselves for guidance and approval—which opens the door to codependency and other toxic relationship dynamics.

WHAT IS MIRRORING?

When I started digging into this work and realized I was a compulsive people-pleaser, I wondered... *How does a people-pleasing personality develop?* One idea that hit home for me was that of mirroring. Mirroring is when adults and caregivers *accurately reflect* a child's expressed thoughts and feelings. This reflection leads to the child's experience of acceptance and validity.[4]

Over time, the child will internalize this *accurate reflection* and enter adult life with self-acceptance and self-awareness. This self-awareness can be seen as the individual's awareness of what they contribute to the world. They will generally experience social acceptance and competence.

But what happens when children are not mirrored accurately? Some-

[4] Jena and Ed Bloch, "Mind Matters - Parental Mirroring Provides Child Sense of Self-Worth," Lawrence Journal-World, 2011, https://www2.ljworld.com/news/2011/dec/05/mind-matters-parental-mirroring-provides-child-sen/.

times, children may become conceited and overconfident in a redemptional effort to feel okay. Other children will struggle with an inability to identify and express their authentic selves. To get approval from parents and peers, they will fabricate identities. Because of a lack of self-esteem, they will withdraw socially.

When parents are trapped in their own struggles with identity, they can fail to provide accurate reflections for their children. Some parents may struggle with intimacy or are too involved in their own inner world to consider their children's emotional needs. This lack of mirroring can be subtle, yet traumatic for the child, leading to loneliness or a lack of self-worth.

As children, we're not equipped with the capacity to deflect or run away from our experiences mentally or physically. We absorb everything into our emotional body. We believe that the way the people in our lives treat us is the way we deserve to be treated—and we have no way of knowing if someone is afraid of intimacy or if they are a narcissist. So, when we are ignored, or we have our feelings invalidated; if someone is irritable or treats us abusively, we believe there's something wrong with us. This becomes the emotional signature we carry into adolescence and into our adult lives.

CODEPENDENCY

As noted, a common trait in people-pleasers is a low self-esteem and a feeling of not being "enough." This feeling of "not-enoughness" fuels codependent behavior, so you only experience the world as it relates to other people. You search for validations of your "enough-ness" in the world outside yourself, seeking to control and fix other people's problems. You are so focused on everyone around you, *you* become your own blind spot. You forget your own needs and desires... and even your mental and physical health.

Codependency, according to Psych Central, is "… a way of behaving in relationships where you prioritize someone else over you, and you assess your mood based on how they behave."[5] It often involves a sense

---

[5] Crystal Raypole, "What Are the Signs of Codependency?," PsychCentral, 2021, https://psychcentral.com/lib/symptoms-signs-of-codependency#what-codependency-is.

of forgetting where you end and the other person begins. The more you support the other person, the more they lean on you, and after a time, it becomes difficult to disentangle yourself.

A research review conducted in 2018 shows that there are four major themes involved in codependent behavior:

1. self-sacrifice

2. a tendency to focus on others

3. a need for control, which may fuel conflict, and

4. difficulty recognizing and expressing emotions.

There is overlap between people-pleasing behavior and codependency…many sources list people-pleasing as a sure-fire sign of codependent relating.

Codependency/Counter-dependency Paradox

Codependency is an unbalanced way of relating. When we show up in this way, we attract unbalanced people. Just as the yin/yang symbol shows the symbiotic relationship between black and white, and shadow and light, a codependent person will attract a counter-dependent person. Counter-dependency is a shiny term for a fear of intimacy. Someone who is counter-dependent dreads the idea of ever needing to depend on anyone, the heart of which is an inability to trust. The mantra of the counter-dependent person is "I don't need anyone."
We can oscillate between the two extremes, moving from codependency to counter-dependency after we've spent years giving way too much of ourselves.

Ten Common Signs of Codependency

There are a few tell-tale signs of codependency, and a lot of them are similar to those of people-pleasing. If you are codependent you:

1. have a deep-seated need for approval from others.

2. take on more work than you can handle, to either earn praise or to lighten a loved one's burden.

3. avoid conflict.

4. minimize or ignore your own desires.

5. experience changes in your mood that reflect how others feel, rather than your own emotions.

6. feel guilt or anxiety when doing something for yourself.

7. idealize partners or loved ones, often to the point of maintaining relationships that leave you feeling unfulfilled.

8. fear rejection or abandonment.

9. have a tendency to apologize or take the blame in order to keep the peace.

10. will often decide for others or try to "manage" loved ones.

With codependency, the need to support others goes beyond what's considered healthy. The codependent ends up overextended, exhausted, confused, and sometimes even abused by the counter-dependent. It is our responsibility to overcome this unbalanced behavior and take care of ourselves. We can do this by releasing responsibility for the actions of the people around us. It takes work, but eventually you'll be able to see that the actions of the other folks in your life occur *in spite of* you, not *because of* you. You'll also stop expecting people to be different than they are, thus freeing yourself emotionally.

This shift in consciousness is imperative if you desire to have healthy relationships in your personal and professional life.

CHAPTER 4

Recognizing Toxic Relationships & Behaviors

*Sometimes your heart needs more time to accept
what your mind already knows.*

—Unknown

Wow... I just got used....

I'd entered a business transaction without drawing up a contract (which was unlike me) because I'd been charmed by the owner of a company (I'll call him Liam). Liam had a vision of changing the world for the better, and he flattered me about my work. I'm a Graphic and Web Designer, and was excited about Liam's vision and mission for his company. I thought I could trust him, that he would honor his word. Boy, was I wrong! I spent months building out his company's brand and packaging design with the promise of equity at the end, and when it came time to collect, Liam was unavailable and dodging my emails and calls. More months went by as I waited for him to figure out the logistics he told me were in the way of issuing my equity. I poked and prodded to get a timeline in place. Six months of nudging and being dodged later, I realized he did not intend to issue my equity. I felt like an idiot—I'd allowed myself to be exploited. After a few months of trying to get paid in cash for the work I'd done, and eventually threatening to take collection action, I got a fraction of the invoice and we went our separate ways... but not before

Liam guilt-tripped me about how this was "not like me."

Lesson learned: there are opportunistic people out there who do not have your best interests at heart. They can sniff out a people-pleaser *a mile away*. I didn't know my sensitive, empathic nature made me an easy mark for predators. My parents, God bless them, had seen my big heart and tried to shelter me from the harsh world, but as I started navigating the real world myself, I got many cold, hard slaps to the face.

I'll never forget the day I learned about toxic relationships, narcissistic personality disorder, and the narcissist/empath dynamic. My rose-colored glasses fell off and I saw everything as it truly was. It was a profound—and heart-breaking—experience. I realized that Liam was a narcissist. One red flag I ignored with Liam was that after every encounter with him, I left feeling confused, foggy, unbalanced. I'd forget everything we'd talked about. For someone with a near-photographic memory, this was odd. I learned later that this is a symptom of an unhealthy relationship behavior called "love-bombing," (see below for definition/details) which narcissists use (consciously or unconsciously) to throw people off. It doesn't just happen in romantic relationships; love-bombing can happen in friendships and business interactions, too.

Many people-pleasers, myself included, will ignore red flags in favor of focusing on the other person's positive traits. This can get us into dangerous situations, so it's important to be realistic, practice discernment, and recognize signs of an unhealthy relationship.

TEN SIGNS OF AN UNHEALTHY RELATIONSHIP

We all have our quirks, and we all do unhealthy things sometimes. We can learn to relate better by recognizing unhealthy signs and shifting to healthy behaviors. If you notice unhealthy dynamics in your relationship, don't ignore the signs. Unhealthy dynamics can grow into abuse.

Here are ten signs you're in an unhealthy relationship dynamic:

1. Intensity right off the bat

Things can get intense when someone expresses huge emotions for you or over-the-top behavior that makes you feel uncomfortable early in your relationship. If someone seems to rush the pace of the relationship or gets obsessive about wanting to see you all the time or talk to you all the time, that is a red flag.

As noted, "love-bombing" can happen in any kind of relationship. It happens when a person tries to influence you by using big displays of attention or affection. They will:

- compliment you incessantly.
- lavish you with gifts or promises.
- bombard you with phone calls and text messages.
- want your undivided attention and seem needy.
- try to convince you that you are soulmates (yes, even in friendships).
- want commitment from you *right now.*
- get upset when you establish boundaries.

If you are being love-bombed, you will feel overwhelmed by the other person's intensity and feel unbalanced when you are around them (and especially once they have left). It may feel intoxicating at first, but you will also feel anxious, like you're "waiting for the other shoe to drop." Pay attention to this anxiety. Remain attuned to your intuition. It's important to be grounded so you don't get swept away by love-bombing tactics.

2. Possessiveness

While we all feel jealousy, it becomes toxic when the other person uses their jealous feelings as an excuse to keep tabs on you or lash out at you. Possessiveness happens when the other person gets upset that you're texting or talking with someone else, wrongly accuses you of flirting or cheating, or goes as far as stalking you. People who are possessive will often downplay their toxic behavior by saying that they're overprotective or have powerful feelings for you. If you notice this behavior, address it. If the person is willing to listen to you and back off a bit, you might be able to salvage the bond. If they get defensive and try to blame you for their behavior, exit stage left.

3. Manipulation

This behavior can be hard to spot, because it comes packaged in subtle, passive-aggressive actions. When someone is manipulating you, they are trying to control your actions, decisions, and conduct. You'll know you're being manipulated if someone tries to convince you to do things that make you uncomfortable, gives you the silent treatment until they get their way, or tries to guilt trip you into doing things.

4. Isolation

This is another subtle toxic tactic…it starts off with someone wanting to spend more one-on-one time with you, and it builds into them demanding that you not spend time with certain people. You become alienated from most of your friends, family members, and even work colleagues. The toxic person will ask you to decide between spending time with them or with your friends, or make you question your judgment of your friends or family members. You can end up feeling like you depend on this person for affection, love, and even money.

5. Sabotage

A toxic person will keep you from doing the things you want to do. They will discourage your ideas, downplay your achievements, try to ruin your reputation, and even sabotage your opportunities. Saboteurs will talk behind your back, try to convince you that people are out to get you (while playing both sides), condescend to you, try to wreck your confidence, or even start rumors about you.

6. Belittling

This is when someone says and does things that make you feel bad about yourself. This can range from criticizing you to calling you names or saying rude things about the people you're close to. Or they can belittle you by making jokes at your expense about things they know are a sore spot, and laughing it off because "you're too sensitive." Over time, you will question yourself and your own judgment, and your confidence in yourself and your abilities will dwindle.

7. Guilt trips

Have you ever had someone blame you for something out of your control and try to make you feel bad about it? That is guilt tripping. They may try to manipulate you into doing things you're not comfortable with by telling you you'll make them happy or that they'll be hurt if you do not do it. This behavior might even delve into an extreme realm, whereby they will threaten to hurt themselves if you don't do what they want or if you don't stay with them.

8. Volatility

When you're with someone volatile, you're walking on eggshells, wondering when the next explosion will come. Volatility is when someone has a strong, unpredictable reaction to something that makes you feel scared, intimidated, or confused. Your relationship might feel like a rollercoaster with huge ups and downs. You never know what's coming next. They might lose their temper over small things, have major mood swings, or lose control of themselves...yelling at you, threatening you, or even getting violent.

9. Deflecting responsibility

A toxic person never takes responsibility for their actions, and may even try to blame *you* for their awful behavior. They have excuses for all their unhealthy conduct, and it's always someone else's fault they behave as they do. They own none of it, instead blaming their ex, their parents, their alcohol or drug use, the government, or mental health issues for their unhealthy behavior.

10. Betrayal

Being disloyal and telling lies is straight up toxic behavior. A toxic person might act differently around others than they do with you, may share your private and sacred information with others, or may leave you out or cheat on you.

If you recognize any of these unhealthy dynamics in your relationship, don't ignore them. If you ever feel you are in a dangerous situation, trust your intuition. Reach out for help. See the Resources section at the back of this book to get yourself out of danger.

You don't ever have to tolerate people who treat you poorly.
It doesn't matter if it's a friend, a family member, or a partner.
It doesn't matter how long you've known them for
or how nice they may have been to you in the past.

—Daniell Koepke

THE NARCISSIST EMPATH DYNAMIC

Many people-pleasers are empathic people. They can sense the feelings and emotions of the people around them and take on a lot of outside energy. Many people-pleasers and empaths have come from difficult, even abusive situations where they had to be on guard all the time and learned to read the energy of those around them.

As I mentioned before, early in my life, I felt the emotions of everyone around me strongly. I figured out ways to mirror others and make them happy, which made me feel happy, too. Little did I know this tendency was codependent, and left me open to be taken advantage of by narcissists. I got into some strange, hurtful friendships and romantic relationships with people I thought had my best interests at heart, but discovered later that they were only around me because of how I made them feel. The moment I started setting boundaries or expressing my true feelings, the relationships blew up.

Once I was on a trip with a girlfriend to Costa Rica, and had decided to end the romantic relationship I was in with a partner. My friend recommended I read *Women Who Love Too Much* by Robin Norwood. On the plane ride home, I read the entire book. The book made many things click for me and I had a lot of Aha! moments reading it. I realized *why* I was attracted to certain types of relationships and friendships and noticed patterns in my style of relating to others that weren't healthy.

I then discovered the work of Dr. Christiane Northrup,[6] who spoke at length (and wrote books about) narcissistic abuse and the empath-nar-

---

[6] Christiane Northrup, *Dodging Energy Vampires: An Empath's Guide to Evading Relationships That Drain you and Restoring Your Health and Power* (New York: Hay House, Inc., 2018).

cissist dynamic. Even *more* things clicked into place for me. This began a two-year-long deep dive into therapy and different healing modalities to heal from the narcissistic abuse I'd suffered throughout my life, to re-program my mind with healthier ways of relating, and to learn how to set boundaries. I stayed single for almost two years while I did this work, vowing never to enter the same types of relationships again. Having done this work, I can see a narcissistic personality a mile away and know to keep my distance. I can also sense when I slip into people-pleasing, or codependent behavior and bring myself out of it. It's my hope that the following information will be helpful for you to discern between healthy and harmful ways of relating.

So, let's get into what empaths and narcissists are, and dive into the toxic dynamic that can happen between these two personality types.

Who Is an Empath?

In a YouTube interview with Michael Sandler, Dr. Christiane Northrup gives a perfect description of who an empath is:

> An empath is somebody who walks into a room and feels the room with their body as the sensory instrument, and often we can't tell the difference between where we end and they begin. But there's more...many of us are very, very old souls, so our very energy field begins to be an air purifier for the room. The problem is if you're born this way as a little kid and your parents do not understand your sensitivity, you think that something is wrong with you. And that's not the case at all.

Empaths can feel big emotions out of the blue, crying or becoming tired, because of the energy they've taken on. If people around you (the empath) don't understand why this happens, they can label you as being "too sensitive." Empaths are drawn to the healing arts because we *feel into* the people around us in a way that most others cannot. We can see, sense, or feel where emotional energy is trapped in other people and how to release blockages. Empaths are lovely—and loving—people who want to make a positive difference in the world and help others. We want to do the right thing and can't imagine hurting others.

The energy field of an empath is strong—and what happens when we turn on a light? We attract moths. Enter the narcissist.

Who Is a Narcissist?

The word "narcissist" gets thrown around a lot these days to describe anything from someone who posts too many selfies on social media to an outright sociopath. Narcissists are people with Narcissistic Personality Disorder (NPD), a mental condition that encompasses a few characteristic traits—most notably a lack of empathy, an inflated sense of self-importance, and troubled relationships.

According to the 5th edition of the *Diagnostic and Statistical Manual of Mental Disorders,* there are nine criteria for this personality disorder. The official narcissist definition for NPD includes:

- a grandiose sense of self-importance

- a preoccupation with fantasies of unlimited success, power, brilliance, beauty, or ideal love

- the belief they are special and can only be understood by, or should associate with, other special or high-status people or institutions

- the need for excessive admiration

- a sense of entitlement

- the display of interpersonally exploitative behavior

- a lack of empathy

- the envy of others or a belief that others are envious of them

- a demonstration of arrogant behaviors or attitudes.[7]

Even though we are armed with this information, it can be tricky to spot a narcissist. According to therapist, relationships expert, and author Marianne Vicelich:

Many people who consider themselves to be excellent judges of character can have a difficulty in seeing a self-centered person for who they really are. Their true identity may eventually reveal

---

[7] American Psychiatric Association, *Diagnostic and Statistical Manual of Mental Disorders: DSM-5.* (5th ed 2013).

itself to some, but to most others, narcissists may appear driven, charismatic, ambitious, disciplined, and even fun. They also display attributes of glibness, feelings of high self-worth, pathological lying, proneness to boredom and emotional unavailability.

The Toxic Dance Between Empaths and Narcissists

One of the worst false narratives that empaths are sold is that narcissists must have been hurt in childhood. We can't imagine hurting others, manipulating them, or trying to have them do our bidding. It's the furthest thing from our nature. With the cliche that "hurt people hurt people" floating around, we think that if we love a narcissist hard enough, we can help them heal. This creates a toxic cycle wherein the empath gives and gives to the narcissist, believing that one day their love and care will transform them, when they are just giving the narcissist an endless supply of energy off of which to feed. The narcissist is a black hole—the more you give, the more they take. They seem to have "malignant intuition" that allows them to see the wound in you and know what you've always been wanting to hear. So, you get love-bombed with sweet nothings until you are snared—and the mind games begin. You'll be drawn in and pushed away in a cat-and-mouse game that will have you acting in ways you never thought possible. And as soon as you question them or assert your boundaries, you will get cut off.

How to Protect Yourself and Still Help Others

The first step in protecting yourself is recognizing that people like this exist. One in five people have a personality disorder of some type. So, twenty percent of the people you come in contact with could be a narcissist or have a similar mental imbalance that could be harmful to you. I know... *wow.*

The second step is to hone your intuition and examine how you *feel* after interacting with certain people. After spending time with a narcissist, you may feel drained and/or confused. If interacting with a narcissist, suddenly you might feel like you're going to fall asleep, when before you got there, you had pep in your step. I've been in interactions where I'm digging my nails into my thigh to keep my eyes open. This is a surefire sign you are with an energy vampire/narcissist. On the flip side, after interacting with a person who has a healthy mental state and demeanor, you will feel energized. Being a people-pleaser, you're inclined to be focused outwardly. When you bring your awareness inward, the insights you gain will amaze you! Your body is intelligent and will always let you know when something isn't quite right (or when it's great!).

CRABS IN A BUCKET

While not every troublesome person is a narcissist, there are people in this world who *don't* want the best for you. This may come as a shock. Sometimes the people closest to us can turn on us. Some people will be attracted to your light and reject you when they get too close. They can't handle how bright your light is.

Have you heard the analogy of crabs in a bucket? The story goes that if there are a bunch of crabs in a bucket and one crab is trying to climb out, the other crabs will band together to pull that crab back into the bucket. This is the same dynamic that can happen with the people around you. They might seem to support you, but as soon as you try to better yourself, they will do or say something to bring you back down. Rather than support you on your way up, they would prefer you remain on a level they can relate to. This behavior often presents because seeing you striving for new heights triggers something in them—perhaps they always wanted to do what you're doing, or they feel like if you achieve your goal, you will abandon them. Rather than talk to you about how they feel, they might make passive-aggressive digs about you or your goal. So, you have a choice—you can confront the person about their behavior and open a dialogue, or you can distance yourself. Sometimes you'll come back together, sometimes the space between you will remain.

I've been heartbroken after realizing certain people I thought would be by my side forever turned out to be my greatest naysayers. It's amazing what happens around you when you make big moves (or even small moves) toward your goals. The sad fact is there are people who benefit from you being a people-pleaser and an over-giver. You don't want to see it because you see the best in everyone. I get it. Watch what happens when you set boundaries. You can tell by people's reactions whether they were benefiting from you overextending yourself.

SOMETIMES REJECTION IS PROTECTION

Rejection is one of the biggest fears of people-pleasers. We try to please others to avoid it! But rejection is a part of life. *You will never please every single person. It doesn't matter how good your intentions are.* Rejection isn't a bad thing. Sometimes the universe conspires in ways that make it look like you are being rejected, but really, you are being protected from misaligned, potentially harmful people and situations. One of the hardest lessons I've had to learn is that no matter how good a person you are, no matter how much you try to understand others, be empathetic, or reach out to help, some people just will not like you. Ever. Ouch.

For the longest time, if someone didn't like me, I took it personally, and would try to win them over. I'd come at them from different angles, trying to understand and empathize with them, trying to find some common ground… all to no avail. I'd end up defeated and exhausted. Sometimes I made things worse.

One day, I woke up with fresh eyes. I saw that the people I'd been trying to win over were, in fact, just miserable. They were like that with everyone, not just me. A couple of them despised me *because* I was happy and friendly. That was a head-shaker. It sunk in after a while that some people weren't happy within themselves, and there was nothing I could do to fix that. In fact, *it wasn't my place* to fix it. The things I was trying to fix in other people were the same things I needed to fix in myself—I didn't like admitting that, because I identified as a happy-go-lucky person. But in the depths of my being was a cavernous despair I was afraid to explore, and these people were reflecting this back to me. Woah…

This epiphany started the process of me calling back all the energy I had been funneling into everyone else and their stuff. It hit home for me that I was fighting a losing battle, that these people didn't want my help, anyway.

TOXIC RELATIONSHIPS ARE STRESSFUL

Whether it's at home, with friends, or at work, your relationships play a key role in your mental and emotional health. Being part of dysfunctional or toxic relationship dynamics can take a toll, and if your mental and emotional health are out of balance for an extended period, can affect your physical health as well. Chronic stress can wreak havoc on the body. According to healthline.com, stress can cause:

- headaches
- increased depression
- heartburn
- insomnia
- rapid breathing
- weakened immune system
- increased risk of heart attack
- high blood sugar
- pounding heart
- high blood pressure
- stomach and digestive issues
- fertility problems
- low sex drive, and
- tense muscles.[8]

STAY IN YOUR OWN LANE

One of the most empowering things you can do for yourself is to "stay in your own lane." This is the biggest learning curve for people-pleasers who are so used to extending themselves in a million different directions all day long.

"Stay in my own lane? What does that even mean?"

Make sure you're living your own life—not someone else's. Having been engrained in people-pleasing habits, you've been used to hiding your true feelings, not speaking up for yourself, and not rocking the boat in order to spare other people's feelings or make them happy. If you are more concerned with the feelings of other people than you are about your own, you will make decisions "outside your lane." You can't stay on your

---

[8] Ann Pietrangelo, "The Effects of Stress on Your Body," HealthLine, 2019, https://www.healthline.com/health/stress/effects-on-body.

own, God-given path if you are more concerned with someone else's feelings (or problems). To stay in your own lane means to put all of that focus on yourself, your health, your life and your goals.

"But that sounds selfish! Won't that turn me into a narcissist?"

I know it might feel selfish, but I promise you, staying in your lane is not selfish. In fact, it's a healthy way of being and relating. You look after you and fill your cup, and you let other people live their life and figure their stuff out. Then you can come together as two whole people and relate in a balanced way, instead of being codependent. Staying in your lane is allowing other people to be responsible for their own feelings and lives. If someone is:

- hurt that you're not available
- hurt that you don't want to go on a date with them
- upset that you decide not to use their business services, or
- disagrees with you…

… their feelings are not yours to worry about. Now, we want to treat everyone with respect, kindness, and compassion in everything we do. But if you show up and treat people well and they're still upset with you, please don't spend your time worrying about that. They're adults and can sort out their own feelings. You don't have to explain why you don't want to do something or feel guilty for saying "No" or having boundaries. You don't owe anyone your time, attention, or presence if it's not in line with your path or it drains you.

Take all the mental energy you would spend worrying about what that other person is thinking and channel it toward things that add to your life—like working on your goals, cooking good food, or spending time with your loved ones. Stay on your own path, in your own energy, and in your wholeness. Take responsibility for your own feelings and emotions, rather than focusing on everyone else's feelings.

You are not responsible for other people's reactions. As long as you are showing up in a moral, respectful way, you can sleep well at night. You can't control anyone else's reactions. Not everyone sees the world in the same way. They are coming at their situation from their own experiences, wounding, and expectations, and might not empathize with you. That's okay. Stay in your lane, hold firm to your boundaries, and move on. We'll cover more about boundaries in Chapter 8.

LIVE AND LET LIVE

Now, on to a section that I know some people will not like (see how I'm not taking responsibility for your reaction to this?).

Sometimes you have to let others fail and fall. It's a part of their life journey, learning, and growth. I know this can be hard for parents, because you want your kids to succeed in the world and never get hurt. But staying in your lane allows your child to explore the world and figure out how to be autonomous. You can be there when they need you, but if you try to do everything for them or shelter them too much, they may feel smothered and rebel. The same goes for other family members, friends, and business colleagues. You might think you're helping by trying to do everything for them, but this robs them of a chance to shine and become empowered.

When you're doing everything for everyone else, you rob yourself of your own chance to shine. The world doesn't get to experience the true you when you're burnt out or overextended. Chances are, if you're trying to hold the entire world up by yourself, there isn't a lot of room for you to explore your own creativity, personal growth, business ideas, etc. So, staying in your lane means:

- coming to terms with the fact that you are only one person and can only do so much.

- focusing on yourself, your feelings, and your life more than on those of everyone else.

- having boundaries and enforcing them.

- allowing others to take responsibility for their own feelings.

- remembering you can't control other people's reactions.

- realizing you've got to let other people make mistakes and live their own lives so they can learn, grow, and become empowered.

Your energy and time are precious. Don't let anyone drag you off your path into negativity.

TEN SIGNS OF HEALTHY RELATIONSHIPS

As you make healthier choices for yourself and create boundaries, you will experience a shift in perspective around your daily interactions. You'll see which ones are adding to your life and which ones are not. It's important to have compassion for yourself and for others during this process.

A healthy relationship doesn't mean a "perfect" relationship. We all have our moments, but in a healthy relationship, you will feel comfortable to discuss things, agree to disagree and be respectful of each other.

Here are ten signs of a healthy relationship:

1. A comfortable pace

A healthy relationship moves at a pace that is comfortable for both people. You won't feel rushed or pressured in a way that makes you uncomfortable. In any new relationship, you're going to want to spend a lot of time with each other, but it's important to find a balance between any relationship and time spent alone or with others.

2. Trust

Because you feel respected and seen, trust comes easily. You don't have to worry about what the other person in the relationship is doing, or whether the other person will betray you or hurt you. They respect your privacy and will never feel the need to put you through a "test" to prove your loyalty.

3. Honesty

You will express your true feelings and opinions without worrying about how the other person will react. You will feel comfortable telling the other person about your thoughts and your life and they will listen to you. They may not always like what you have to say, but you can agree to disagree and/or they will react to disappointing news with compassion.

4. Independence

It's important that each person in a relationship also has their own lives and time to do what they want to do outside of the relationship. In a healthy bond, the other person will support your hobbies and passions, and encourage you to spend time with your friends, family, and co-workers with no play-by-play of every detail. You will be supportive of the other person's hobbies, passions, and bonds outside of your relationship. Then you'll have things to talk about when you are together!

5. Respect

You value each other's beliefs and opinions and appreciate each other as individuals. You feel safe and comfortable to set boundaries and are confident the other person will respect those boundaries. You cheer for each other's wins, support each other, and appreciate each other.

6. Balance and Equality

Both of you put the same amount of effort into the success of your relationship. When you both want something different, you compromise, and one person's preferences aren't dictating the direction of the relationship. You feel like your needs and desires are just as important as the other person's. Sometimes, one person might give more than the other. There is no keeping score of who did what, because you both know that things will balance themselves out down the line.

7. Kindness

You are loving to and empathetic with each other. Your kindness is reciprocated by your partner and vice versa. You do things you know will make the other person happy and make them feel seen and cared for. You show compassion for the other person, listen to them, and show interest in the things they care about.

8. Taking Responsibility

Both people in a relationship must own their words and actions. You can admit when you've made a mistake, apologize, and avoid placing blame. You take responsibility for the effect your words and actions had on the other person, even if it wasn't your intention, and you try to make positive changes for the benefit of each other and your relationship. When one person owns up to something, the other person never shames them. You work together to make things right.

9. Healthy Conflict

Conflict is expected in any relationship. What makes a healthy bond is the way the conflict is handled. You should be able to discuss issues and handle disagreements without judgment or condemnation. Healthy conflict means you're able to work together to get to the root of the issue and deal with it before it festers and turns into a bigger problem. There is no yelling or belittling in a healthy conflict.

10. FUN

A healthy relationship should feel like home, a place where you can have fun and be yourself. You should want to spend time together and enjoy each other's company. You can let loose and have a good time. No relationship is going to be fun 100 percent of the time, but the good times should outweigh the bad.

THE FRIENDSHIP AUDIT

It's said that you become the average of the five people you spend the most time with. I can attest to this, and invite you to explore this yourself. Take a good look at the five people you've spent the most time with over the last month. Are they tracking toward accomplishing their goals? Are they positive people? Do they support you? Be honest as you do this exercise. You can even write everything out in a journal. Which of these people are adding to your life? Which are taking more than they are giving? Our relationships should be reciprocal. We should get as much as we are receiving out of our interactions. If there is an imbalance, that needs to be rectified.

If you looked around at the people you spend the most time with, would you say you are surrounded by people who support you? Do your friendships bring you joy? Security? Opportunities for mutual growth? Do you have good communication? Are you able to talk about the hard things?

Have you thought about this before? As we grow and move through life, it may not occur to us that we can curate our friend circles. So often we'll stay in friendships and other relationships because we've known someone for a long time. Familiarity can trump growth and expansion, and even joy in our relationships as we sink into comfortable ruts. After some time, people with whom you were close can feel like strangers as you each venture down your individual paths.

There's something to be said about a beautiful, long-standing friendship that has stood the test of time. I see a lot of articles out there about friendship audits that encourage you to cast aside friendships like you would an old pair of shorts. Just like anything worth having, a good relationship of any kind takes work and investment. What I would like to encourage you to do today is to assess the closest relationships in your life and see how they make you *feel*. After being focused on pleasing others for a long time, you may not have ever made time to check in with yourself about your feelings *about* the relationships you keep.

Here are some prompts to help you reflect on your friendships and see which ones are healthy and which ones might not be. Explore these questions with a single individual in mind at a time, and be honest with yourself.

- Do I feel close to this person? Why or why not?

- Do I feel I can trust this person with my innermost feelings and thoughts?

- Am I comfortable asking this person for help?

- Do I enjoy this person? Does this friendship bring me joy?

- Would I feel comfortable letting this person know if they'd hurt my feelings? If not, why not?

- Does this friendship help me through difficult times? Is this person someone I would call if I were in pain or experiencing suffering?

- Do they love me for who I am?

- Do they listen without trying to fix everything for me?
- And—do I want to be friends with this person?

Examining Your Friendship Group

Below are some questions pertaining to your whole friendship group. I've found these to be interesting to ponder, and invite you to explore for yourself.

- Which traits do all my friends have in common? Why do I (subconsciously) seek these traits in my friends?
- What is the glue that holds my friendships together? Why did I become friends with these people?
- Does this group inspire me? Challenge me? Encourage me to grow?
- Does my heart feel safe within my group of friends?
- Who has always been there for me through thick and thin?

Look in the mirror...

- What kind of friend am I?
- What do I expect out of friendships in return?

Our friendships can be our greatest mirrors. Sometimes friendships trigger us and bring out emotional baggage we thought we'd dealt with. Each time we're triggered, we're invited deeper into ourselves and our emotional world, and are offered an opportunity to transmute energy into something life-giving for ourselves and our friends. We're being given a chance to have a tough conversation, and to express our feelings, our boundaries, and our expectations—to open up a dialogue. Each time we open ourselves to these types of experiences, we learn and we grow. A key to learning how to stay calm when we're triggered and have the opportunity to learn from our relationships is self-awareness. In the next chapter we'll go over some different ways that you can cultivate strong self-awareness and learn how your mind operates, so you can navigate your relationships and their lessons with more ease.

CHAPTER 5

Cultivating Self Awareness & Analyzing Your Behavior

Self-awareness is the ability to take an honest look at your life without any attachment to it being right or wrong, good or bad.

—Debbie Ford

The first step in breaking free of the habit of people-pleasing is to cultivate a practice of self-awareness around your overly accommodating behavior. In order to change behavior, you need to be aware of when it's happening *in the moment* so you can make decisions from a place of calm presence rather than an emotional reaction. I'm sure you've heard a lot of buzz about "being present." There is a reason all the sages talk about this *ad nauseam*. Learning to bring yourself into the present moment is *powerful*. When you are present with what's happening right now and are calm, you can watch your body's reactions, be cognizant of your thinking process, and make better decisions.

Think about it... when you're all jacked up, fearful about what someone might think of you when they ask for a favor, you're going to say "Yes" before you take time to think. When we're caught up in emotion, our logical mind gets clouded. Ever say something in a rage you later regret? It's the same thing. When we're emotional, our sympathetic nervous system switches on. As one blogger at Harvard Health Publishing said, it "triggers the fight-or-flight response, providing the body with a burst of energy so that it can respond to perceived dangers."[9] With people-pleasing, the perceived danger is that the other person will not approve of us if we say "No." Thinking about the outcome creates anxiety, which triggers a flood of emotions, which switches on the sympathetic nervous system and puts us into fight-or-flight mode. That burst of energy propels an impulsive "Yes" out of our mouths to protect us from this danger. Then, when we get home, away from the danger, our parasympathetic system pumps the brakes, calms us down, and we regret what we've done.

So how do you stop this cycle? With practice, discipline, and simple relaxation and mindfulness practices, you can keep your parasympathetic "rest and digest" nervous system activated, so you can remain calm in high-pressure situations and make better choices for yourself at any given moment.

THE NERVOUS SYSTEM AND MENTAL HEALTH

I know, you didn't pick up this book for a biology lesson, but this is really cool! You see, people-pleasers and perfectionists often struggle with anxiety. We worry, and sometimes can't shut it off. This mental stress is taxing on our bodies, causing insomnia, muscle tension, rapid heart rate, fatigue, gastrointestinal issues, sweating, and headaches.

Why do people-pleasers feel anxious? It stems from a core fear: we think we're inadequate, defective, or unlovable—and we're afraid others already know this or will find out. Some schools of thought[10] call this "Imposter Syndrome," and it can leach into every aspect of our lives. To play it safe, we stick to what we're good at. We work hard (often too much). We try to be agreeable, which leads to stuffing our feelings, needs, and opinions (especially if we think they're disagreeable or inconvenient). We're conditioned to be hypersensitive to the possibility of being criticized, abandoned, or rejected. So, when healing from people-pleasing, you will also be healing your anxiety and nervous tendencies.

---

[9] "Understanding the Stress Response," Harvard Health Publishing, July 6, 2020, https://www.health.harvard.edu/staying-healthy/understanding-the-stress-response.

[10] Arlin Cuncic, "What is Imposter Syndrome?," Very Well Mind, updated on October 22, 2022, https://www.verywellmind.com/imposter-syndrome-and-social-anxiety-disorder-4156469.

As I journeyed toward better mental health, I stumbled upon information on the vagus nerve and exercises you can use to stimulate this nerve and relax the body. These exercises have been *life-changing* for me, and I'd like to share them with you.

What is the Vagus Nerve?

The vagus nerve is the longest nerve in your body. It connects your brain to many important organs throughout the body, including the intestines, stomach, heart, and lungs. The word "vagus" means "wanderer" in Latin,[11] which represents how the nerve wanders all over the body and reaches various organs. The vagus nerve is also a key part of your parasympathetic "rest and digest" nervous system. It influences your breathing, heart rate, and digestive function, all of which have a tremendous impact on your mental health.

An important aspect of vagus nerve function is called *"vagal tone."* Vagal tone is an internal biological process that represents the activity of the vagus nerve. Increasing your vagal tone activates the parasympathetic nervous system, so having a higher vagal tone correlates to your body being able to relax faster *after stress.*

It's almost like yin and yang. The vagal response reduces stress. It reduces our heart rate and blood pressure. It changes the function of certain parts of the brain, stimulates digestion, all those things that happen when we are relaxed.[12]

—Dr. Mladen Golubic, M.D.

In 2010, researchers discovered a link between high vagal tone, positive emotions, and good physical health. So, the more you increase your vagal tone, the more your physical and mental health will improve. You can measure your vagal tone by tracking certain biological processes such as your heart rate, breathing rate, and heart rate variability. (I'll leave it to you to do your own digging on that.) The point I'm getting at is that

---

[11] Jennifer A Clancy et al., "The Wonders of the Wanderer," National Library of Medicine, 2013, https://pubmed.ncbi.nlm.nih.gov/22848084/.
[12] "Doctor Explains How to Relieve Anxiety Instantly Using Your Vagus Nerve," Power of Positivity, 2017, https://www.powerofpositivity.com/relieve-anxiety-vagus-nerve/.

mental and physical health are interconnected. When you can calm your nervous system, you cultivate greater self-awareness and intuition so you can respond differently *in the moment* to whatever life throws at you.

The following practices stimulate the vagus nerve and activate your parasympathetic nervous system, which can relax you. Journal your experiences with these practices—and see what changes you notice in yourself after you've been practicing for a while.

Cold Exposure

According to Wim Hof, a Dutch motivational speaker and extreme athlete also known as The Iceman, exposing yourself to cold regularly can lower your sympathetic "fight or flight" response and increase parasympathetic activity through the vagus nerve.[13] It's also a great way to train your mind to get used to uncomfortable situations. I go outside in cold temperatures with minimal clothing often, and I take cold showers. You can ease yourself into cold exposure by sticking your face in ice-cold water, or finishing your shower with at least thirty seconds of cold water. See how you feel. Then work yourself up to longer periods of time.

Deep, Slow Breathing

You may have had someone tell you to "take a deep breath," or perhaps you have given this advice to others. Deep, slow breathing stimulates your vagus nerve and has been shown to reduce anxiety. Most people take about ten to fourteen breaths per minute. Reducing this to six breaths per minute is a great way to relieve stress. Deep breaths come from your diaphragm, meaning that during a deep belly breath, your stomach should expand. Allow your exhale to be longer than your inhale, as this is the key to stimulating the vagus nerve and reaching a state of relaxation. For example, you could breathe in for a count of four and breathe out for a count of eight. Below are a couple of simple breathing exercises you can try.

Straw Breath

This breathing technique is as simple as it sounds. I use this technique

---

[13] Wim Hof, "Vagus Nerve Stimulation," Wim Hof Method, https://www.wimhofmethod.com/vagus-nerve-stimulation.

often when I feel myself getting wound up, and it always cools my jets. Take a deep inhale with your diaphragm, allowing your stomach to expand outward. Then, either exhale through a straw or purse your lips like you are blowing through a straw. Try not to push your breath out; allow it to leave your lungs slowly. See if you can notice a change in your body after a few breaths.

4x4 Breath (Box Breathing)

This breathing technique is one that the U.S. Navy Seals use to stay calm and focused before and after intense combat. It's simple and you can do it in five minutes. Here's how:

1. Find a comfortable chair or place to lie down.

2. Inhale for four seconds, allowing your belly to expand.

3. Hold the air in your lungs for four seconds.

4. Exhale for four seconds, emptying all the air from your lungs.

5. Hold your lungs empty for four seconds.

Repeat this for five minutes or until you feel relaxed and refocused.

Singing, Chanting, Humming, or Gargling

Your vagus nerve is connected to your vocal cords and the muscles at the back of your throat. Singing, chanting, humming, and gargling can activate these muscles and stimulate your vagus nerve, and this has been shown to increase heart-rate variability and vagal tone.

The same goes for socializing and laughing, which reduce cortisol and stimulate the vagus nerve. Laughter has been shown to increase heart rate variability and improve mood, and vagus nerve stimulation often leads to laughter as a side effect—so you can create a beautiful and positive cycle within yourself by using your voice and connecting with others!

Meditation

Meditation is my favorite technique for relaxation and feeling connected to life. Little did I know when I started meditating that I was also stimulating my vagus nerve and increasing my vagal tone.

New to Meditation?

No problem! A great place to start is with mindfulness meditation. This is a simple practice of focusing the mind on a particular object, thought, or activity to train attention and awareness, and achieve a clear, calm, and stable state. You can start today with a simple, five-minute practice. Just know going into this that it takes time to train your mind to do something new, so when you first do this, *you will become distracted.* Especially in this modern age of technology, we've become unfocused. That's okay! The more you practice, the more you will focus, and the longer you will sit each time. Go into your practice with an open mind and no agenda, and allow yourself to just *be in the present moment* with whatever happens. It can be helpful to keep a meditation journal and log your experiences each time you meditate. Then you can look back on your progress and celebrate your achievements.

A Simple, Five-Minute Mindfulness Practice

In the beginning, I've found it helpful to set a timer, so your mind knows how much time you'll be practicing, and you know you'll be notified when it's finished. This will give your mind fewer things to wonder about.

- Find a spot where you will not be distracted for five minutes and where you can sit comfortably.

- Put your phone on airplane mode. Set a timer for five minutes.

- Close your eyes. Observe your breathing without trying to control it.

- Every time you inhale, say "IN" in your mind.

- Every time you exhale, say "OUT" in your mind.

- When your mind wanders, bring it back to the task at hand. Be careful not to judge yourself. There is no such thing as completely "shutting your mind off." Remember, this is a *practice.*

- Continue this until the timer runs out.

The more you practice, the more you will notice your nervous system calming down. With consistent practice, you'll notice you can focus on tasks for longer. Your memory might even improve! You'll see how much your mind operates on autopilot. According to Emma Young, science and health journalist and author, "Current scientific estimates are that some 95 percent of brain activity is unconscious."[14] Ninety-five percent!

If you'd like to try out some different guided meditations, you can find some good ones at www.doitforyoubook.com/resources.[15]

Exercise

Exercise increases levels of a chemical involved in brain cell growth, which boosts the release of the hormone dopamine, the "feel good" hormone. It's also been shown to stimulate the Vagus nerve, which may explain its positive effects on our mental health. Many brain health experts recommend exercise as their number one piece of advice for optimal brain health.

There are many exercises you can try, from walking to weightlifting, to high intensity interval training to yoga asanas, dancing and even gardening. What's important is that you exercise in ways you enjoy so you stick with it, and so you ease into new routines and listen to your body.

Massage

The vagus nerve can also be stimulated through massage. There are many videos out there showing you how to perform a vagus nerve massage on yourself, but I would recommend visiting a Registered Massage Therapist who can carry out this procedure for you without causing injury and can show you how to do the massage techniques yourself properly. If you do decide to follow along with a video, please be gentle with yourself and be aware of how your body reacts to any type of pressure. Stop if you feel sharp pain or pinching.

*

[14] Emma Young, "Lifting the Lid on the Unconscious," New Scientist, 2018, https://www.newscientist.com/article/mg23931880-400-lifting-the-lid-on-the-unconscious/.
[15] Vanessa Ooms, "Supplemental Material for Do It For You," Do It For You, 2022, http://www.doitforyoubook.com/resources.

JOURNALING FOR SELF-DISCOVERY AND EMOTIONAL ALCHEMY

When you were younger, did you keep a diary hidden under your mattress? For me, my diary was a place to confess all of my thoughts and emotions without fear of judgment or punishment. It was my safe place where I could escape the tribulations I faced. It felt good to release all that angst onto the paper and get it out of my head. After a good session with my diary, the world seemed clearer.

Though you may have stopped keeping a diary in adulthood, the concept and benefits still apply. These days, it's called journaling, and it's simply writing out all of your thoughts and feelings so you can get them out of your head and see them from a different perspective. Journaling can help you gain control of your mental health and process your emotions healthily. Writing my pages each morning helps me gain clarity and prioritize my day. When I experience an acute emotional response to something, writing about it helps me understand my emotions and the thoughts that come with them and express it all in a healthy way. It gives me space to process what's going on before I respond, so I can ensure I'm acting in a way that is healthy for all parties, rather than acting on emotional instinct.

Benefits of Journaling

One of the best ways to deal with overwhelming emotions is to express yourself. Journaling can help you cope with anxiety and reduce stress by:

- helping you to express fears and concerns and see things from a different perspective.

- helping you dump tasks from your brain in order to organize and prioritize.

- tracking any symptoms day-to-day so you recognize patterns and triggers and learn ways to manage your emotions better.

- identifying negative thought patterns and giving you an opportunity to redirect your mind toward positive affirmations.

- identifying the source of stress and problems so you can work to remove the problems that bring anxiety into your life.

Approaching a Journaling Practice

It might seem overwhelming to sit down with an empty notebook and think of what to write. Here are some tips to make the process more approachable and enjoyable:

- **Try to write every day.** This will help you get into the practice of writing. Set aside even five minutes each day at the same time that will be your writing time. Make it a priority.

- **Make it easy.** Keep a pen and paper handy so you can write out your thoughts when the mood strikes you. If that doesn't seem doable, there are many journaling apps you can put on your phone or computer. My personal favorite is called "Journey."[16] I've been using it for years, and I love being able to journal on my phone whenever I feel inspired or feel I need to clarify situations for myself. I intersperse my phone journaling with paper journaling, depending on where I'm at and how I'm feeling.

- **Allow yourself to write and draw whatever comes to mind.** Your journaling doesn't need to follow a set structure. This is your sacred, private space to express yourself, *in whatever way feels right in the moment.* Don't worry about messy writing or spelling mistakes. Resist the urge to edit your writing. Because I'm a perfectionist, one of my mentors challenged me to write five pages per morning without lifting my pen from the paper, then putting the book away and not looking at it again until the next day. It felt great to vent everything and then leave it. If (with my permission) you looked through my journals, you'd see varied pages with small writing, huge and messy writing, scribbles, more detailed drawings, pressed leaves, pages ripped out, and pages that became wavy because of the tears they had collected. I share this with you, hoping it will encourage you to just let it rip with your journaling!

Journaling has been (and still is) one of my all-time favorite tools for self-expression and introspective work. It amazes me how I can start out writing about a present problem, and end up connecting with a part of

---

[16] "Sanctuary for Your Mind & Soul," Journey, https://journey.cloud/.

my childhood or a part of myself I'd long ago forgotten. Keeping a journal helps you create order when your world is chaotic. Journaling can help you make sense of dreams, provide a healthy outlet for powerful emotions, and act as an organizational tool when you've got too many things streaming through your mind. It's such an individual activity that you won't know just how journaling can help you until you sit down and put pen to paper (or use a journaling app).

TYPES OF JOURNALING

While I encourage free-flow journaling, I understand that when you're just getting started, sometimes it's nice to have a jumping off point. There are a couple of ways to approach journaling. One is doing stream-of-consciousness writing, or what I call a "brain dump." Another is to use journaling prompts to get your juices flowing.

Stream-of-Consciousness Writing (Brain Dump)

Stream-of-consciousness journaling is the method I use most often. It's a transcript of your thoughts—like you're having a conversation with yourself, but on paper. Stream-of-consciousness has no structure. You don't need a topic sentence or thesis statement. All you do is write every passing thought as it comes to mind. When I write, I don't ask myself, "What should I write about?" I sit down, take a few breaths, and write the first thought I become conscious of. Then the next one. Often, I'll start by writing about how delicious my coffee is, gushing about how cute my dog is, or writing about a prevalent emotion in that moment—and go from there. Often, my thoughts are scattered. Sometimes one sentence is about one thing and the next is about something else.

You can think of stream-of-consciousness writing as a monologue. A blogger named Jestine at Rediscover Analog compared this writing style to a fast-speaking character who is also the narrator of a film.

Don't Know What to Write?

Sometimes, you'll sit down with your notebook and draw a blank. When this happens, start with "I don't know what to write" over and over, and soon you'll write about something else. There is always something to ramble on about, and the beautiful thing about stream-of-consciousness is that it doesn't have to make sense. It doesn't have to have structure or sound like anything in particular. As I mentioned earlier, it's a transcript of the random thoughts bouncing around in your mind. Write like no one is watching.

Using Journaling Prompts

While you can learn about yourself by reviewing your day, journaling can take you much deeper when you use prompts to direct the flow of your mind. Journal prompts offer specific themes and topics to focus on, which can be helpful if you feel blocked or you have unorganized thoughts and don't know where to start. There are a variety of journaling prompts for different areas of life that can help you discover more about yourself and process your emotions. To get you started, here are some examples:

- Explore an opinion or two you held in the past but have since questioned or changed. What led you to change that opinion?

- When do you trust yourself most? When do you find it harder to have faith in your instincts?

- What values do you consider most important in life (honesty, justice, altruism, loyalty, etc.)? How do your actions align with those values?

- What do you appreciate most about your personality? What aspects do you find harder to accept?

- Describe one or two significant life events that helped shape you into who you are today.

In the next Chapter, we'll get more in-depth with journal prompts to take you deep into self-reflection.

MINDFULNESS IN DAILY LIFE

Not everyone has time to dedicate to a sit-down meditation practice. That's okay! We live busy lives. The cool part is you can practice mindfulness throughout your day, no matter what you're doing. The whole point of mindfulness is to *"be here now,"* in the present moment, with whatever you are experiencing. Here are some examples:

1. Doing the dishes—feel the warmth of the water on your hands. Notice how the soap bubbles reflect light. Watch the little rainbows on top of each bubble and how the bubbles float around your hands and the dishes. Take in the shape, weight, and color of each dish. Think about what it took to create that dish and have it land in your home. Imagine how far that dish must have traveled to get to you. Feel gratitude because you have dishes.

2. Snuggling with a pet—feel the warmth of your furry friend's body against yours. Notice all the different colors in their fur and the amazing number of hairs on their body. Admire their ears, eyes, nose, mouth, and teeth. Look at their little paw pads and nails. Watch their ribs rise and fall with each breath. Beautiful!

3. Enjoying a cup of coffee or tea: sink into your favorite spot. Turn off the TV and phone. Feel the comfort of the surface supporting you. Feel the warmth of the mug transfer into your hands. Watch the steam billow up from your mug. Admire the way it dances and hangs in the air. Take in the fragrance of your drink. Enjoy its flavor, holding the warm liquid in your mouth for a moment before swallowing it. Thank your body for allowing you this experience. Pure gratitude.

Another way to practice mindfulness is to check in with yourself throughout the day. How are you feeling? What is going on in your mind? You might be surprised at the thoughts that pop up when you adopt an Observer's mind.

OBSERVER MIND V. AUTOPILOT MIND

Have you ever been so caught up in your thoughts you forget why you walked into a room? If you're like most of us mere mortals, your answer is "Yes." We have so many automatic thoughts whizzing through our minds regularly, we can become consumed by them and not even notice—until, for example, we get to a destination and realize we can't remember the car ride. Like I mentioned earlier, it's said that ninety-five percent of our thoughts happen below our conscious awareness, in our subconscious mind. That's a lot of habitual and automatic thinking! When we use Observer Mind to bring conscious awareness to our habitual strings of thoughts, we can learn a lot about ourselves and our subconscious programming, as well as make different (and healthier) choices in our lives.

Observer Mind is a simple, powerful, technique that has been around for centuries and is used to cultivate focus and reduce stress. It's the practice of becoming aware of our thoughts. Cognitive Behavioral Therapy (CBT) outlines the process like this: an activating event (A) happens. You have a belief (B) about the event, which causes a consequence (C). The consequence is an action, a thought, or an emotion.

The same event could mean different things to different people. For example, a rain storm might cause a bride a lot of grief, whereas a farmer might be grateful for the water after a dry spell. It's not an event itself that is necessarily good or bad, but our *beliefs* about that event that makes it so in our minds. By recognizing the A-B-C sequence that happens in your mind that leads to your conclusion of, for example, rain being good or bad, you can transform your thinking process and create new beliefs and meanings.

Be compassionate and patient with yourself as you practice Observer Mind. As you start to observe your automatic and repetitive thought patterns, you may notice thoughts that are disempowering or that stem from negative past experiences. Try not to judge these thoughts, but instead consciously follow them. When you notice a thought that doesn't serve you, follow it to the next thought, then the next, then the next with an open mind. You may be surprised where the thoughts lead you. Stay present, patient and open during this process. The more you discover about your own thinking, the more you will be able to build a hypothetical "map of your mind," which will help you get to know yourself deeply and also show you where you can start making positive changes for yourself.

Let's consider how we can use Observer Mind to cultivate new beliefs that are healthier and serve us better. For example, let's say that a friend hasn't returned your text in what you consider to be an appropriate time frame. Do you allow automatic thinking to control your reaction, or do you allow Observer Mind to direct your thoughts?

Automatic Thinking:

1. Activating event (A) happens: my friend hasn't texted me back yet.

2. Belief (B): they're ignoring me.

3. Consequence (C): I get angry and decide to ignore them, too.

Observer Mind:

1. Activating event (A) happens: my friend hasn't texted me back yet.

2. Belief (B): they're ignoring me.

3. Consequence (C): I get angry...then *observe* my reaction.

4. New Belief (B): I remind myself that it's not about me.

5. New Consequence (C): I calm down and call them to see if they got my message.

This process might seem simple, but I promise you, it's profound. When you stop yourself mid-reaction and *choose* a different reaction and belief, you feel empowered and in control of your mind and life. Since people-pleasing behavior is often unconscious and automatic, in the next section, we'll dive back into the Ten Signs You're a People-Pleaser, using Observer Mind this time. Learning to see your habitual thought patterns and their unconscious source will help you choose ways of behaving that are fair and empowering for you. Be gentle with yourself as you move through this process of self-evaluation. You didn't become a people-pleaser overnight. It will take time to undo habitual patterns of thought and behavior and replace them with healthy ones.

Meditation and the Observer Mind

At one time, I had used meditation for several years to calm my mind, but that was it. When I started using meditation as a tool for self-discovery, everything changed. I noticed patterns of thought and behavior, how they worked together to form different emotions, and my reactions to these emotions. I felt like I was on a scavenger hunt, finding clues buried in my subconscious mind that would help me understand the puzzle of my psyche, see how my mind was programmed, and change that programming. I started slowly. I was flying by the seat of my pants, but eventually a meditative process emerged that incorporated not only the Observer Mind technique, but delved even deeper. It goes something like this:

1. I notice when I'm feeling a negative emotion.

2. I sit down and meditate on the negative emotion. I get into Observer Mind and watch what's happening inside my mind, without labeling or judging. I watch, noticing all the narratives that pop up.

> a. i.e., I feel annoyed because my friend (let's call her Sarah) just called and vented for an hour and a half, and she never asked me how I was doing. Now I'm exhausted. This frustrates me and hurts my feelings. Why? Because I feel like her emotional dumping ground. I feel like my feelings don't matter, like Sarah doesn't care about me. She doesn't care about me because I don't matter. *She doesn't care about me because I'm not good enough.*

3. Once you've drilled down to the core feeling underneath the presenting emotion (i.e., "I'm not good enough"), you can see where this idea came from in the first place…if you're open to the process. If you remain still long enough, old memories might float to the surface that carry the same emotional charge. As I allowed memories to surface I noticed they had the same energetic signature—each perpetuated the idea that *I'm not good enough.*

4. Write down what you've just experienced in a journal or in your journaling app to release the experience from your mind.

DO IT FOR YOU

It can also be interesting to go through your notes at a later date.

5. Be gentle with yourself. It can be painful and overwhelming. Remember to stay in Observer Mind during this process, resisting the urge to judge your inner narrative or experience.

6. Use one of the self-soothing techniques in Chapter 9 to calm yourself after navigating this emotional territory.

7. Resolve to take a different action next time you are in a similar situation. An example might be: "Next time I'm on the phone with Sarah and I notice she is rambling on and I am feeling ignored, I will interrupt her and tell her I have to get off the phone." OR, "When Sarah calls, I can tell her I only have fifteen minutes to talk right now. When the fifteen minutes is up, I will end our conversation."

There is more information for you in Chapter 8 on how to say "No," and have boundaries so that you can be proactive in life and keep your energy intact throughout your day.

ANALYZE THE WHY

The shadow is a moral problem that challenges the whole ego-personality, for no one can become conscious of the shadow without considerable moral effort. To become conscious of it involves recognizing the dark aspects of the personality as present and real. This act is the essential condition for any kind of self-knowledge.[17]

—Carl Jung, Aion (1951)

Now we're getting into some tough love and shadow work. If you want to make significant, lasting changes in your life, look at WHY you behave in certain ways. Have you ever had a moment where you said something awful or agreed to something you didn't want to do, on impulse, that you regretted later? Afterward, you might have felt ashamed, and asked your-

[17] Carl Jung, Aion: Researches Into the Phenomenology of the Self (Routledge & Kagan Paul Ltd, 1959).

self, "Why did I just do/say that?"

That "Why?" question indicates a blind spot. Even though you may rationalize or justify your behavior, your lack of control in the moment shows you there is another part of your personality that lives beneath the constructed idea of who you are. This is your shadow self.

Much people-pleasing behavior stems from our "shadow self," a term coined by renowned Swiss psychiatrist Carl G. Jung, that describes aspects of our personality we choose to reject or suppress.[18] We all have aspects of ourselves we don't like, or that we think other people won't like, and those aspects get pushed down into our subconscious psyches. It is this collection of repressed aspects of our personalities that Jung referred to as our "shadow self."

In this section, we'll look at the Ten Signs You're a People-Pleaser and analyze WHY you behave in these ways. You get a subconscious payoff from every action you take, so let's explore what your payoff is for these behaviors. Is there a healthier way you can get those needs met?

Grab your journal for this part and explore each topic below. As you read through, can you add examples of "Payoffs" and "Healthy Alternatives" that pertain to your own life? Be thorough and blunt with yourself about the payoffs, but be careful not to shame yourself. This exercise cultivates awareness so that you can acknowledge these behaviors and move forward in a healthier way.

TEN SIGNS YOU'RE A PEOPLE-PLEASER REVISTED

1. You pretend to agree with everyone.

Listening to other people's opinions, even if you don't agree with them, is a fantastic social skill. Where it can become toxic is when you agree (or pretend to agree) with everyone around you so you don't rock the boat. This can end up with you doing or saying things against your values, which can make you seem inauthentic.

- **Payoff:** I feel accepted and people like me; I make people around me happy because I agree with them; I get to avoid the

---

[18] Jack E Othon, "Carl Jung and the Shadow: The Ultimate Guide to the Human Dark Side," High Existence, August 7, 2020, https://www.highexistence.com/carl-jung-shadow-guide-unconscious/.

conflict that would come from a debate; I make them feel heard and acknowledged, which makes them see me as a friend.

- **Healthy Alternative:** Respectfully disagree (i.e., "I respect your opinion on this, but I disagree. I believe _____.") Doing this will earn you respect, even if it is rattling for the other person at first. You can practice this with a trusted friend. Get them to pretend they hold a view you disagree with, and practice using this line until you feel comfortable with this language. Then take what you've learned out into the real world. It will feel uncomfortable at first, but the more you face this fear, the more confident you will become.

2. You feel responsible for how other people feel.

Being aware of how your actions make other people feel is a healthy way of relating. However, if we think we have the power to make someone else happy, that is a problem. We are not responsible for other people's feelings. It's important that we learn to stay in our own lane, look after our own emotions, and allow others to take responsibility for theirs.

- **Payoff:** If I fix their problem, I will make them happy and they will approve of and accept me. I'll get an ego boost from saving the day. Maybe they'll tell their friends about the good thing I did and they will like me, too.

- **Healthy Alternative:** Listen with empathy and compassion to the other person while resisting the urge to jump in and fix the problem. Acknowledge that they are a grown person and can take care of themselves. Offer to help if there is something they can't do on their own, but don't offer to do things they can do for themselves. Healthy boundaries empower you both.

3. You apologize often.

Apologizing when you've done something wrong is healthy. But there's a difference between owning something you did and apologizing for something that doesn't require an apology just to make the other person feel better. You don't have to apologize for being yourself or for disagreeing with someone. Frequent apologies can point to a bigger problem. We'll address this later on in the book.

> • **Payoff:** If I apologize first, maybe this will just go away. If I apologize, they'll see me as a good person and I can avoid conflict.

> • **Healthy Alternative:** When you've done something that warrants an apology, own it. But catch yourself when you want to apologize "just because." Do you need to say "I'm sorry," or are you doing it as a reflex?

4. You feel guilty or mean when you set boundaries.

Perhaps you feel selfish if you do anything for yourself that interferes with you showing up for someone else, or you feel guilty for saying "No" to someone who needs you. Being helpful and kind is admirable, but extending yourself to the point of burnout isn't good for anyone. Then you get resentful and don't show up in wholehearted service like you'd want to. What kind of gift is that? It's important to find a balance between taking care of yourself and extending yourself to others.

> • **Payoff:** If I say "Yes," I won't have to upset them and can avoid conflict. If I say "Yes," I'll be able to be their superhero and save the day. They'll see me as a good and selfless person.

> • **Healthy Alternative:** Take some time to reflect on what is being asked of you. Do you have the bandwidth to take it on? If you don't, say "No" using the "No" Scripts in Chapter 8. Maybe, for example, you don't have the energy to go to that dinner. You can say "No" without guilt because there will be other opportunities to get together, and people will respect your boundaries.

5. You go to great lengths to avoid conflict.

Perhaps you don't disagree with people (but then talk behind their back). Maybe you say "Yes" to something, but later fake an illness to get out of it. Or maybe you lend money to someone you know will never pay it back and then beat yourself up for it later.

> • **Payoff:** If I agree to this, I can avoid the stress of confrontation and the possibility of disappointing the other person or

having them disapprove of me. They will remember me as a nice, agreeable person.

• **Healthy Alternative:** Practice disagreeing. Disagreeing with someone doesn't mean you have to raise your voices or get into a fight. It's a healthy exchange between two unique, adult humans where each might learn something from the other. Get comfortable with the fact that conflict is unavoidable, and that it's not the end of the world. You may disagree, negotiate, and debate...and be respected for it. As suggested earlier, practice disagreeing with a family member when you do disagree. Practice expressing your viewpoints and know that *you do not have to take responsibility for anyone else's reactions.*

6. You expect yourself to be perfect and hold yourself to high standards.

People-pleasers want to make the people around them happy and be accepted. This outward extension of energy is a symptom of something deeper... a disapproval and unacceptance of ourselves. We make high standards for ourselves to justify disapproving of and not accepting our true selves.

• **Payoff:** I hold myself to high standards and strive for perfection, so my boss/parent(s)/spouse/friends will approve of me and/or admire me.

• **Healthy Alternative:** I accept myself as I am, flaws and all. I know no one is perfect, including me, so I can relax and know I am doing my best every day. Refer to the section on Mirror Work and Positive Affirmations in Chapter 9 to assist you with this process.

7. You can't say "No."

We've all been here before...someone asks us to do something and we say "Yes" before we check our calendars or check in with ourselves to see if we want to do the thing or can do it. Then we stress about making it happen (among the bazillion other things on our plate) or try to figure out a way to back out of it.

- **Payoff:** Saying "Yes" makes me seem reliable and responsible. If I say "Yes," this person will see that they can count on me, and I get a little dopamine hit from being a hero.

- **Healthy Alternative:** Pause. Check in with yourself before you say "Yes." Check your calendar to see if you have time and make sure you're not double booking yourself. Ask if you can sleep on it and get back to them. Think about whether you want to do this thing. Does it align with your values, schedule, and/or goals? Know that it's okay to say "No" after you've said "Yes!" Check out Chapter 8 for tips on saying "No" and some scripts that you can implement today.

8. You're a "fixer."

You are a beautiful, compassionate soul who doesn't want to see anyone suffer. That's wonderful. But every person walking this earth is going to experience suffering, and there's nothing we can do to stop it. So, rather than trying to be a superhero and fix everyone's problems, learn to just be there for others during trying times. Help if asked, but don't take it upon yourself to fix other people's problems. Doing this can disempower the other person and tax you. No one wins.

- **Payoff:** If I'm able to fix their problem, I get a dopamine hit from completing the task *and* from being needed. Involving myself in this person's life also allows me to distract myself from my own problems and/or procrastinate on my own goals. If I make them happy, that will make me happy! (Note that this attitude is making the other person your project).

- **Healthy Alternative:** Use your empathic skills to hold space for this person and listen to what they are going through. Often, being an engaged listener is all people want, anyhow. Recognize that not everyone needs or wants you to jump in or fix their problems. Sometimes they just need to talk things out. Allowing them space to talk and process things and come to their own conclusions empowers them and releases you from the burden of feeling the need to fix their problem. Ask the other person, "Do you want to vent, or would you like advice?"

9. You've become resentful and burnt out.

You feel exhausted by all the demands on your time and erupt in anger anytime someone asks you to do *one more thing*. It can feel like no one cares about you or your needs and everyone just takes from you. You feel like others only want to be around you to get something from you.

> • **Payoff:** When I'm the martyr and the victim, it makes me feel important. Doing everything for everyone else helps me hide the fact that I don't actually trust anyone to look after me and my needs. There is no need for me to take responsibility for what is happening in my life. I get to blame the "greedy and thankless *other people*" for how burnt out I am and don't have to admit that it was my choice that landed me in this predicament. I get attention from the people around me and get to be validated by the support people offer me. The problem with this payoff, though, is that you are giving other people the power over your life and your wellbeing.

> • **Healthy Alternative:** Realize that *you also matter.* Set aside time and resources to pursue the things that matter to you. Taking care of yourself is essential, because if you're giving from a depleted place, it will not be good for anyone. Spend time with family and friends in environments where you don't need to be helping and just enjoy their company. Notice when you want to jump in and help someone and take a couple of breaths…step back and remember, this person can do things on their own. You can empower them by encouraging them to take on tasks and challenges themselves while you support them from the sidelines.

10. You don't admit when your feelings are hurt.

It happened again. Your friend Joan overstepped and hurt your feelings, and rather than say something, you clammed up and stuffed your emotions. It might seem like it's not worth confronting her about it (maybe she'll think you're being too sensitive or it might start a fight over nothing). It's easier not to say anything…

> • **Payoff:** If I don't admit that my feelings are hurt, I get to avoid

confrontation and whatever fallout may follow it. I don't let Joan see how vulnerable I feel. I can show her I'm tough, that I'm the bigger person, and she can't get to me. I get to feel superior and avoid conflict.

• **Healthy Alternative:** Have a conversation with Joan as soon as she does something that hurts your feelings, rather than stuffing it down and having it explode later. It takes practice, but you can say something at the moment like "You may not have meant this to be hurtful, but when you said/did this, it hurt my feelings and I wanted you to know this." This may feel uncomfortable the first few times you try it, but often you'll be surprised by the other person's response. The first time I tried this out with a friend, she teared up and apologized. She didn't know how her actions were affecting me and promised to do better and be more aware. I've also had the opposite response from people who diminished my feelings, but I took that as an opportunity to validate myself and my own feelings—to self-soothe, as we'll talk about in Chapter 9.

You've just completed some pretty intense work! Please take time to decompress. When you're ready, let's move on to the next Chapter.

CHAPTER 6

Getting Reacquainted with Your True Self

Finding yourself is not really how it works. You aren't a ten-dollar bill in last winter's coat pocket. You are also not lost. Your true self is right there, buried under cultural conditioning, other people's opinions, and inaccurate conclusions you drew as a kid that became your beliefs about who you are.[19]

—Emily McDowell

People-pleasing creates a false "self," an appeasing persona and mask that you put on to interact with the world. You think this false self is protecting you, but it's not. It's blocking you from forming deep connections with others. Before we jump into this Chapter, let's come into this moment, take a few deep belly breaths, and *take off the mask.*

Take off everyone's expectations of you.

Take off what you think you should be.

Take off the shame of not measuring up.

Take off all the layers of who you have been.

Come home to the center of your being where it's quiet, and answer these questions:

[19] "Emily McDowell Quotes," GoodReads, https://www.goodreads.com/quotes/9586181-finding-yourself-is-not-really-how-it-works-you-aren-t.

What kind of person are you?

I am _____.

I am _____.

I am _____.

I am _____.

I am _____.

I am _____.

What are your values?

My values are: _____

_____

_____

_____

_____

_____

_____

_____

I know these things about myself because:

_____

_____

_____

_____

_____

_____

_____

_____

If I didn't care what other people thought about me, I would:

_____

_____

_____

_____

_____

_____

_____

_____

_____

If I had no fear, I would:

_____

_____

_____

_____

_____

_____

_____

_____

If I were really being honest, I would say:

_____

_____

_____

_____

_____

_____

_____

_____

If I had no other responsibilities, I would:

_____

_____

_____

_____

_____

_____

_____

_____

_____

If I were 100 percent free to be myself, I would:

_____

_____

_____

_____

_____

_____

_____

_____

If I had the freedom to explore anything I wanted, I would:

_____

_____

_____

_____

_____

_____

_____

If I truly followed my heart, I would:

_____

_____

_____

_____

_____

_____

_____

_____

If I told them what I really thought, I would say:

_____

_____

_____

_____

_____

_____

_____

If I put myself first, I would:

_____

_____

_____

_____

_____

_____

_____

If I had more time, I would:

_____

_____

_____

_____

_____

_____

_____

_____

I really don't like doing:

_____

_____

_____

_____

_____

_____

_____

_____

I really enjoy doing:

_____

_____

_____

_____

_____

_____

_____

Describe a few things that make you happy:

_____
_____
_____
_____
_____
_____
_____
_____
_____

Describe something you dreamt of doing when you were younger:

_____
_____
_____
_____
_____
_____
_____
_____
_____

Describe something you dream of doing now. Big or small! All your dreams are relevant.

_____
_____
_____
_____
_____
_____
_____
_____

These things nourish my soul:

(The real stuff. Try not to talk yourself out of anything here.)

_____

_____

_____

_____

_____

_____

_____

_____

Great job! You just did some deep work. You may have a lot of emotions swirling inside you right now. Take a time-out. Make yourself a warm beverage and/or head out into nature to reflect on everything that came up. Please don't brush past what you've just explored. Give yourself the gift of time to integrate the truths you just unearthed.

LIFE REVIEW

Before we move forward with the next Chapter, let's discuss a life review, or life reconciliation. We think of a life review in terms of something a person does before they pass away so they can find peace. In my experience, though, the life review process is an amazing way to find peace *now*. It can sometimes be a heavy process and a lot of emotions may come up, but if you do a thorough, honest evaluation of your life up to this point and forgive yourself and others, you can reach a place of unshakeable inner peace you can take with you through the rest of your life.

Expression

People-pleasing can steal your life. I know that sounds dramatic, but so many people are robbed of the life they were born to live because of the invisible disease to please. People-pleasing is like quicksand, drawing you into the worlds of others and having you ignore your own desires and needs. These unmet needs don't just vanish; they get stored in our bodies. The emotion people-pleasers fear the most is anger, and it's usually the first emotion to come roaring out when they tap into their own inner world. Why? Well, our unmet needs bubble into resentment, and resentment turns to anger. *Nice people don't get angry,* so people-pleasers rarely express their anger healthily. It just broils inside of them—and like food left too long in a pressure cooker, the anger seeps out in passive aggressive behavior—or the people-pleaser's lid blows right off and they experience psychological breakdown and burnout. It's either that or the pressure is never released and it corrodes our souls. We move farther away from the person we know we can be and we morph into the person we feel others want us to be. As we sink into the belief that *no one will ever get us,* life becomes lonelier and more isolated. If we never get out of the people-pleasing loop, no one ever will *ever* get us—at least not on a deep level—because we never give anyone a chance. Many people-pleasers turn to unhealthy behaviors and substance abuse, to numb the existential dread and loneliness they feel. That's why the first part of the life review is so important.

You've got to give yourself permission to express your emotions. All of them. First off, remember, your anger is not wrong. Anger needs to be felt and released. When we allow ourselves to feel these emotions and release them, they can be healed. Emotions are *energy in motion,* and we need to allow this energy to move. Anger has a purpose. Sometimes anger shows us that we need to take a different action. Or, if we've been complacent, perhaps we need to take action. Sometimes anger shows us where a boundary of ours has been crossed—maybe one we didn't even know existed. *All* our emotions are tools and messengers for us and our emotions will always be what they are.

Rather than trying to control our emotions, it's important to find healthy ways to express them so we don't stuff them and create dis-ease in our bodies. Our physical, emotional, mental, and spiritual bodies are all connected, and when we're blocking energy in, we create disease. *Dis-ease* in the energetic and emotional bodies will filter out into *dis-ease* in the mental body and *dis-ease* in the physical body, as the last manifestation of what's going on in the spiritual body.

The good news is that it only takes ninety seconds for an emotion to pass through our bodies. According to neuroanatomist Jill Bolte Taylor in her book *My Stroke of Insight*:

> *When a person has a reaction to something in their environ-ment, there's a 90 second chemical process that happens in the body; after that, any remaining emotional response is just the person choosing to stay in that emotional loop. Something hap-pens in the external world and chemicals are flushed through your body, which puts it on full alert. For those chemicals to flush out of the body, it takes less than 90 seconds. This means that for 90 seconds you can watch the process happening, you can feel it happening, and then you can watch it go away. After that, if you continue to feel fear, anger, and so on, you need to look at the thoughts that you're thinking that are re-stimulating the circuitry that is resulting in you having this physiological response over and over again.*[20]

Release Emotions

Anger, resentment, loneliness, and isolation are poisons that can do sig-nificant damage to the human spirit and the physical body. We need to move this energy through and express these emotions, release the energy from the body, and move forward. Here are six healthy ways to release difficult emotions healthily:

1. Exercise.

Move your body, sweat it out. Allow your mind to focus on something else so your body can process the emotions and all the energy. You can try running, sparring with a punching bag, doing squats, or throwing firewood around—anything to get your heart pumping.

2. Shake it off.

Literally shaking. Shake your hands, your body. Let everything go. Allow your body to release the energy. When animals in

---

[20] Jill Bolte Taylor, *My Stroke of Insight: A Brain Scientist's Personal Journey* (New York: Penguin Group, 2009).

the wild experience some kind of crazy event, they shake it off and move on. Have you ever seen ducks fighting or dogs having a little tussle? They'll shake it off, release the energy, then go about their animal business. Human beings don't do this. We keep it all inside, make up stories about it, and shove it down so we don't have to deal with it. Shaking it off allows our bodies to release the energy. Remember, it takes ninety seconds for an emotional charge to move through the body, so you'll be feeling better in no time. Try it right now. It does wonders for the body.

3. Write down your angry thoughts.

Transfer your thoughts onto paper. Don't stop, read, or edit your writing. Let it flow. Write everything going through your mind, no matter how gnarly. Then take that paper and rip it up. When we pour all of this energy onto the paper, the act of destroying it works with our subconscious mind to say, "I'm done with this." "I am releasing this." "This no longer serves me."

4. Give your anger a voice.

This works well with any emotion. Find a private place and voice what's going on. Speak out loud all the angry thoughts running through your mind. This practice gets you out of your head and allows you to see your thoughts and emotions from a different perspective—which can shift your mindset. Giving your emotions a name diffuses the power they have over you. So, when you're in the thick of it, just say (as an example), "Whoa, I'm so angry right now. I'm so pissed off; I feel like a freakin' idiot!" Whatever you need to say, just get it out!

There's a reason we phone people up to vent sometimes, but that opportunity is not always available. So, if you can vent by yourself, it might seem crazy, but you will feel much better. This act also shows your psyche that it's okay to feel these feelings and that you are acknowledging them.

And if you need to, scream! Scream into a pillow or go into a forest where there aren't a bunch of people around and let it rip. Cry your eyes out if you need to. A lot of us are uncomfortable with this form of expression. When I started doing this, I was blubbering and stumbling and had coughing fits because I was blocked up and used to never expressing myself. I lived in the forest, so I could just go out and scream! You would be surprised at how cathartic that is. I know, it seems like you're having a tantrum and...you are. Think about what happens with kids when they get angry—they just let it out! They have a tantrum and then they're fine, because they've released the energy. We need some ways to release the energy as adults as well. Allowing ourselves space to express our emotions is so healing.

5. Breathwork.

If you're not feeling like you can go scream somewhere or you're not feeling the dynamic movement, that's okay. Do some controlled breathing. If you're overwhelmed, this will help diffuse the situation and bring you back to your center.

Putting your focus on your breath calms your nervous system. Then, while you're breathing and focused on your breath, see if you can tune in to your body and notice—where does that anger live? Can you visualize funneling white light or healing energy into that spot and diffuse it? It doesn't have to be a big dramatic thing, just allow the energy to flow into that angry place, and diffuse it from the inside out.

6. Progressive Muscle Relaxation.

Progressive muscle relaxation is just tensing and releasing different areas of the body in succession. This gives the mind a job and brings you into the present moment. Start from the face and move all the way down. Tense all the muscles, hold them tight, and then release. As an example, scrunch your entire face, hold for about ten seconds, and let go. Do this with all the muscles in your body, limb by limb. Let yourself turn into a floppy noodle when you relax your muscles, and remember to breathe.

Responsibility

It takes two to tango. A big part of healing from a bad people-pleasing habit is to take responsibility for the part you've played in these toxic dynamics. Did that sentence trigger your ego? Take a deep breath. Doing this uncomfortable work is essential so you can move forward and create real, lasting changes in your life. Take time to ponder your not-so-great memories and the toxic relationship dynamics in your life. Where does your responsibility lie?

- Have you taken on too much at work without asking for a raise?

- Did you expect your dad to respect your boundaries without telling him what your boundaries are?

- Have you been giving too much of your time to a person or organization? Has that been taking time away from things you want to do?

- Did you miss an opportunity to stand up for yourself? As a result, does someone think it's okay to treat you badly?

- Did you hold your tongue when someone disrespected you? Are you now steeped in resentment instead of talking to them about it?

Think about all the areas in your life where you feel overextended, ignored, or taken advantage of. Examine the dynamics in which you've engaged. Some behavior is straight up abusive and you may need to cut ties with that person. Most times, though, we can make changes in how we show up in these relationships that could change the entire dynamic.

Forgiveness

Forgiveness can be a touchy subject. Forgiveness isn't about the other person. It's not about condoning someone's awful behavior or abuse. Forgiveness is about choosing not to live in distress because of the past anymore. Sometimes it's accepting that you may never get an apology and choosing to give yourself the love and care you wished you had received from that person. Forgiveness is releasing yourself from the shackles of pain and haunting memories.

Forgiving others frees you, and forgiving yourself heals you. Go back over all those scenarios you explored while you were taking responsibility for your part in things. Have compassion for yourself because you were doing the best you could with what you knew. Now you know better. Give yourself a hug.

Acceptance

At some point, we have to accept what our life has been like up to this point so we can move forward. It's not easy to accept what we've been through, but we can't change the past. So we might as well learn from what we've been through and use our lived experiences as motivation and fuel to move forward in a healthy, positive way, for ourselves and for the people around us.

Gratitude

Gratitude is a game-changer and can put things into perspective. Chances are that if you've been wrapped up in people-pleasing for an extended period, you've been focused on *lack*—a lack of time, energy, money, and mental space because you've been over-giving all over the place. Being aware of what you're grateful for helps reprogram your mind to focus on the *good* and the *abundance* in your life. A great gratitude practice is to write down five things that you're grateful for every day. They can be small things like your morning cup of coffee. Search through your day and find five things. Thinking of these things you're grateful for as you wind down your day will help put your mind at ease—and maybe even help you sleep better!

CHAPTER 7

How to Stop Caring About What Other People Think

We would much rather be undefined than ordained in traditions that don't fit our curves.
— Mirabai Starr

We all want to fit in, be accepted, and be validated. Sometimes that desire can get out of control, to where we try to please everyone and win people over; losing ourselves in the process. We can spend unbelievable amounts of time and energy wondering about how other people perceive us, with any amount of praise being overshadowed by one piece of criticism.

Why Do We Care?

Caring what other people think of us is an evolutionary adaptation. According to the Smithsonian National Museum of Natural History,[21] in early tribal cultures, joining a group or tribe and being accepted by others was critical to survival. Even though we may not need to live in tribes to survive today, humans are still wired to be social beings, and we crave the companionship and stimulation of others. Thus, gauging how others are

---

21 Smithsonian Institution, "What Does it Mean to be Human?," Smithsonian National Museum of Natural History, last updated July 7, 2022, https://humanorigins.si.edu/human-characteristics/social-life.

evaluating us is natural and unavoidable.

Caring about how our actions impact the people around us plays a crucial role in maintaining meaningful relationships. If you were causing harm to a friend or family member, you would want to know, right? And while it might be uncomfortable once you knew, you would make adjustments to your behavior to remedy the relationship. That said, putting too much time and energy into worrying about what other people think can damage your self-image and mental health. Taking the opinions of others as truth can lead to a vicious cycle of vulnerability and insecurity. Signs you care a bit too much about what others think, include:

- You hold your tongue if your opinion differs from everyone else's.

- You change yourself in response to criticism, regardless of what it is and from whom it comes.

- You apologize, even when you did nothing wrong.

- You let other people decide for you.

- You don't set or maintain boundaries.

- You're a perfectionist.

- Your peace of mind relies on others' approval.

- You rarely say "No."

Care about what other people think and you will always
be their prisoner.

—Lao Tzu

So let's talk about the elephant in the room—Other People's Opinions (OPO's). As we outlined in Chapter 1, a big reason we start people-pleasing is to avoid having anyone think badly of us. I can't tell you how many hours I've agonized over "what-ifs" in my head, only to face the person in question and have everything work out fine. So, let's think about this— is this bogeyman of OPO's something we should fear? Let's break down what an opinion is, and dissect where OPO's come from, so that we can shine a light on this spooky-looking shadow.

According to the online Cambridge Dictionary, an opinion is the idea that a person or a group of people have about something or someone, which are based mainly on their feelings and beliefs.[22]

Note what it says at the end of the definition—"...*based mainly on their feelings and beliefs.*" Interesting. So how do opinions get formed?

Opinions are fascinating, fickle things with many layers and dimensions. The formation of an individual's opinions happens within the melting pot of their psyche. Every opinion is filtered through a person's beliefs, biases, inner dialogue, emotional triggers, experiences, *and their own fears.* So, every person you come in contact with is going to have a unique experience of *who you are.* You may inspire one person, nurture the next, and trigger or put off the next. Every person's experience of you is biased, subjective, and emotional. The craziest part is, you have no control over another person's experiences, triggers, emotions, judgments, opinions, beliefs, or attitudes. You have zero control over what anyone thinks of you, no matter how hard you try to please them. Sometimes, *just being yourself* will make someone dislike you—because something in the way you move through life triggers something in them they do not want to face. If they are not willing to work through their own stuff and look at why they're feeling that way, it's easy to project those feelings onto you. All you can do in such a case is send them love—and move on.

The diagram on the next page shows what I like to call the *filters of bias* that can cloud a person's perception and color their view of you. When you think about people's opinions in this way, you'll see layers that are beyond your control and influence.

The bottom line is that someone else's opinion of you is wrapped up in their own experience. That might sound disempowering, but letting this knowledge sink in will actually allow you to disconnect from OPO's and empower yourself. You will have *healthier* relationships with others, because you will feel confident in yourself and who you are, and won't need to manipulate how other people see you.

---

[22] Cambridge Dictionary, "Opinion," accessed Jun 13, 2022, https://dictionary.cambridge.org/dictionary/english/opinion.

ANATOMY OF AN OPINION

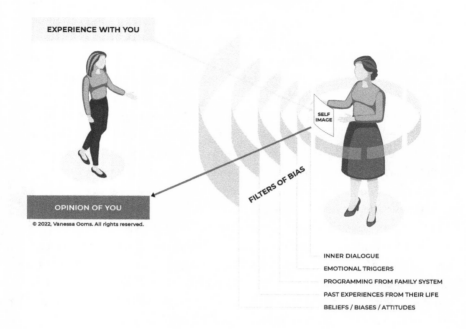

BREAKING FREE OF APPROVAL SEEKING

You've seen how subjective OPO's of you are and how they may not have much to do with you. So, how do we interrupt this cycle of worrying about them? How do we stop caring so much about what other people think of us?

1. Expect and accept that people will have opinions about you.

It's impossible to avoid judgment. Assessing other people is a natural part of human interaction. So prepare yourself. Other people are going to form opinions of you, some of which may be inaccurate. Remember the *Anatomy of an Opinion* diagram you saw above? Remind yourself that other people's opinions are filtered through their own feelings, beliefs and biases, so they may not have an accurate picture of who you actually are in their mind. This will help you let incoming critiques roll off your back.

2. Take control of your feelings.

You do not have to take other people's opinions as truth. Other people may have poor opinions of you, but that doesn't mean that's who you are. While you can't control how other people perceive you, you can lessen your anxiety and worry about it. Learning to be in the moment can help you cope with unwanted thoughts and feelings. Try meditation, yoga, or breathing exercises to bring you into the present moment and back into your body.

Breathe. Remember that *you* control your mind...not the other way around.

3. Don't make assumptions.

Have you ever assumed that someone perceived you a certain way, based on an experience, and then gone home and ruminated over it—even having imaginary arguments in your head? Then, the next time you interacted with that person, you realized you'd been wrong? According to Don Miguel Ruiz, in his book *The Four Agreements:*

> *Making assumptions and then taking them personally is the beginning of hell in this world. Almost all of our conflicts are based on this, and it's easy to understand why. Assumptions are nothing more than lies that we are telling ourselves. This creates a big drama for nothing, because we don't really know if something is true or not.*[23]

Assumptions can be dangerous to our interpersonal relationships. It's important to address issues before they fester into bigger problems. One line I've found helpful in dissolving my own assumptions is this— "Hey, I feel you're feeling _____ about me. Is this true? Or am I making things up?" This opens the door for an honest dialogue and can dispel assumptions before they do damage.

4. Consider the source.

Not all opinions are created equally, and they should not all carry the same weight for you. For instance, a family member telling you how your

---

[23] Don Miguel Ruiz, *The Four Agreements: A Practical Guide to Personal Freedom* (Amber-Allen Publishing, 1997).

behavior is affecting them, or a boss expressing concern with your work can be helpful. Comments from random armchair warriors on the internet…not so much.

5. Realize that people don't think about you as much as you think they do.

Most people are so caught up in their own lives, their own thoughts, and their own insecurities, they don't have time to think about you. You may have blundered in an interview or stuck your foot in your mouth during a conversation, but nine times out of ten, the other person has forgotten about it or didn't think it was a big deal. Let this sink in: *People don't think about you as often as you think they do.* Know this and be free!

6. Recognize that human beings are prone to cognitive distortions.

We are wired to think about the absolute worst-case scenario right out of the gate. It's a tendency of the human condition to blow things out of proportion and spiral into negative thinking. So, you might have had a thirty-minute conversation that was beautiful, but you said one dumb thing and *that* ends up being what you focus on. So, question your thinking. Why are you beating yourself up? Are you worried that the other person is irate and telling other people about it? Is it possible you're making a bigger deal out of this than is necessary?

7. Let go of perfectionism.

Where do these expectations come from, anyway? Who is expecting you to be perfect? There is not one perfect person on this planet. Every single human being is fallible and trying to navigate life on Earth to the best of their ability. So expecting yourself to be perfect is setting yourself up for failure. You'll never be perfect. None of us will. No one has everything 100 percent figured out, and in order to be loved and valued, you don't have to be anything or anyone other than who you are right now. Allow this to sink in. Give yourself permission to be perfectly imperfect. Set yourself free!

8. Get to know your true self.

When you are super solid in who you are, it won't matter as much what people think or say about you, because you know your truth. So, who are you, underneath all the masks? What makes you tick? What do you enjoy doing? What do you enjoy learning about? What do you enjoy talking about? What physical activities do you enjoy? What little things bring joy to your heart? Get to know yourself on a deep level and find a group of people who vibe with the *real you*. Go back over your answers to the questions in Chapter 6. Keep reading them until they're engrained in your subconscious mind. If you haven't gone through the exercise of getting reacquainted with your true self in the previous Chapter, I recommend you do so.

9. Surround yourself with supportive, loving people.

An enormous part of self-improvement is determined by the people around you. They shape your life. Even the simple act of observing other people can affect your mood and motivation. Energy is contagious—all forms of energy. When you are surrounded by people who are positive, motivated, and supportive of you, you will strive to do better in your life. Likewise, if the people around you are stagnating, you will slow down. When you are trying new things in life and sailing into uncharted territory, it's vital to have people in your corner who believe in you and who will cheer you on, particularly in tough times. Your real crew won't compete with you—they'll be happy for you while they are working on their own goals. If you can't find like-minded people to hang out with in person, surround yourself with positive people online. Whether it's a group coaching program or a small Facebook group, you would be surprised at the amount of support you can glean from strangers on the internet!

10. Consider therapy.

Speaking with a therapist can help you to develop skills for coping with criticism and building your self-confidence. Cognitive Behavioral Therapy (CBT),[24] for example, works to build more helpful ways of thinking.

---

[24] Patricia Oelze, "What is Cognitive Behavioral Therapy?," Better Help, August 26, 2022, https://www.betterhelp.com/advice/therapy/what-is-cognitive-behavioral-therapy-definition-and-applications.

You can learn new ways to approach negative feedback and let go of unnecessary stress.

If traditional counseling isn't your jam, there are many modalities that can help you cope with harsh feedback and build confidence:

- **Systemic Constellations Therapy**[25] is an amazing practice that can help you unearth subconscious programs that are getting in your way. Founded by the late German psychotherapist Bert Hellinger, a Family Constellation:

  ...attempts to reveal an unrecognized dynamic that spans multiple generations in a given family...Practitioners claim that present-day problems and difficulties may be influenced by traumas suffered in previous generations of the family, even if those affected are unaware of the original event.[26]

  Though I haven't experienced a full Family Constellation session with multiple representatives, I've gone through two individual Constellation sessions, and the revelations and subsequent transformation in my thoughts, emotions, and life were incredible. If you're interested in this subject, a brilliant book you can read is *It Didn't Start with You: How Inherited Family Trauma Shapes Who We Are and How to End the Cycle* by a leading expert in the field of inherited family trauma, Mark Wolynn.[27]

- **Attachment-Focused Eye Movement Desensitization Reprocessing (EMDR)**

  EMDR is an evidence-based, effective modality designed to treat the traumas that often underlie anxiety, depression, PTSD, phobias, low self-esteem, and many other difficulties.[28] EMDR uses several bilateral stimulations, like eye movements and butterfly tapping, to help clients access memories stored in the subconscious. This mind-body method, when carried

---

[25] "Family Constellation," Hellinger Schule, https://www.hellinger.com/en/family-constellation/.
[26] "Family Constellations," Wikipedia, https://en.wikipedia.org/wiki/Family_Constellations.
[27] Mark Wolynn, *It Didn't Start with You: How Inherited Family Trauma Shapes Who We Are and How to End the Cycle* (New York: Penguin Books, 2016).
[28] "What is EMDR?," EMDR Institute, Inc., accessed on September 16, 2022, https://www.emdr.com/what-is-emdr/.

out by a qualified therapist, facilitates the safe processing of traumatic memory. It has the effect of moving psychological memory to objective memory, desensitizing the memory's impact on the individual's current life.

• Emotional Freedom Technique (EFT)

Similar to acupressure, EFT focuses on the meridian points, or energy hot spots, to restore balance to your body's energy. According to The Tapping Solution website, the basic Tapping technique has you focus on a negative emotion that you're currently feeling while tapping your fingertips five to seven times on nine specific meridian points of the body[29] Tapping on these meridian points sends a calming signal to the brain, letting it know that it's safe to relax.

• Quantum Healing Hypnosis Technique (QHHT®)

QHHT is a technique founded by the late hypnotherapist Dolores Cannon, and involves inducing a somnambulistic state of trance through visualization. Under ordinary circumstances, this state is experienced only twice daily: the moment just before you wake up and the moment just before you fall asleep. Hypnotists have avoided conducting research with subjects in this state because of the often strange and inexplicable results.[30] Starting in the 1960s, Dolores discovered that a powerful, knowledgeable aspect of an individual can be contacted and communicated with when the subject is in this somnambulistic state. This part of ourselves, the subconscious mind, is always present and exists just below the surface of our conscious mind. When the subconscious is accessed and communicated with via QHHT®, spontaneous healings can occur.

There is much research out there now about the subconscious mind and the powers of reprogramming it. We're just scratching the surface.

[29] The Tapping Solution LLC, "Tapping 101," The Tapping Solution, accessed on August 22, 2022, https://www.thetappingsolution.com/tapping-101/.
[30] "What is Quantum Healing Hypnosis Technique?," Dolores Cannon, Accessed on August 29, 2022, https://dolorescannon.com/about-qhht/.

11. Hold off on your judgments of others.

This seems counterintuitive, right? But accepting others can help you let go of worrying about what others think of you. You know the saying, "What you focus on grows?" Well, if you're casting judgments on others, you're going to be hyper-focused on what others think of you. If you know you're giving others the benefit of the doubt, it's easier to assume others are doing the same for you.

When you give others the benefit of the doubt, you'll have a calmer perspective on life. As you practice being kind to others, you'll be kinder to yourself. The judgments we cast on others have more to do with ourselves than they do with the other person. See the diagram called *Anatomy of an Opinion* that I referenced earlier and put yourself on the opposite end. All *your opinions and judgments* are filtered through *your own self-image*, experiences, programming from your family unit, and subjective beliefs. You may not be as objective as you think you are in your assessments of others...and you want others to give you the benefit of the doubt, right? Well, the adage "treat others how you want to be treated" comes in here.

12. Become your own best friend.

Sometimes, before you can find that tribe that vibes with you, you've got to have your own back and be your own best friend. How many of us can say we're our own best friend? For real? Do you have your own back? Often, when we are concerned with what other people think of us, it's because we're judging ourselves. If you observe your inner dialogue for long enough, you'll see that the judgment you fear from other people is the judgment you're placing on yourself. It's easier to see it come from an external source. Then we can blame someone else for being a judgmental jerk, instead of addressing the core problem: *the way we treat ourselves.* When you tweak your inner dialogue to support yourself and become your own best friend, you attract other people who reflect that support back to you. We are attracting reflections of what is going on inside of us. That can be a hard pill to swallow, but that's the red pill that can change everything for you.

You'll learn more about becoming your own best friend and implementing radical self-care in Chapter 9.

HOW TO DEAL WITH CRITICISM

Do it for yourself, not for them. Whatever it is for you, check in with yourself: *Why am I doing this?* Make sure it's something you want to do, rather than something you think others believe you should be doing. When you do the thing that makes your heart sing, do it for you. We seem to think we have a lot of time on this planet. We don't. As we age, time seems to whip by ever faster until we cross to the other side. While you're here, do what nurtures your soul. What makes you happy? What brings depth and meaning to your life? Make time for it, because no one else is going to carve that into your schedule for you. If you face criticism for following your heart, below are some tips to help you deal with it.

Decide Who Gets to Criticize You.

Look at the people around you. Whose opinions matter? Remember, not all criticizers are equal, and some shouldn't even have a seat at your table. Does this person criticizing you inspire you? Do they *see you?* Do they have your best interests at heart? Criticism from a mentor is more valuable and important than criticism coming from an anonymous keyboard warrior on the internet. Set criteria for people who get to criticize you. Forget the rest. The amount of mental energy this will save will amaze you!

Expect to Receive Both Admiration and Criticism.

Putting yourself out there in any way is a double-edged sword. Whether it's standing up for yourself or being the face of a brand, some people are going to agree. Others aren't. But would you rather be judged or ignored?

Whatever happens, the ancient Stoics, those philosophers who believed in the power of positive thinking before it was 'a thing,' remind us not to be carried away by either praise *or* criticism. Remember, any feedback from another person is filtered through the layers of their own experience. Listen, analyze, learn…and move on. Face criticism head on.

> *"There's only one way to avoid criticism:*
> *do nothing, say nothing and be nothing."*
> —Aristotle

While avoiding criticism might provide short term relief, it won't do you any favors. Trying to avoid criticism makes you weak. Worse yet, this behavior will have you withholding your gifts from the world. When you learn to face and receive criticism objectively, you build emotional resilience and give yourself a chance to grow. You can take constructive criticism and learn to do better, or you can face harsh, unconstructive criticism and become firmly rooted in your truth. Either way, when you face criticism, you win.

Seek Improvement, Not Approval.

The only approval you should seek is your own. High-five yourself for your small wins each day. Write them in a notebook and save them. You will be amazed at how much progress you make and how much this simple practice can improve your morale. When you face criticism (notice how I said *when*, not *if*), rather than seeing it as exposing your flaws or as rejection, use it as fuel to better yourself. Taken in the right mind-frame, criticism can help you make self-discoveries. Often we're so wrapped up in our heads, we don't see opportunities for growth or improvement. Viewing things objectively can be a self-development tool. What is constructive about the criticism you received? Challenge your ego's reaction to it. Find the nugget of truth, and let it inspire you to set higher standards and try something new. You might be surprised at the positive changes you experience and the new opportunities that open up when *you* open up to feedback.

If You Can't Control the Sting, You Can Keep It from Swelling.

Criticism stings. Sometimes there's no getting around it. But how you react can mean the difference between the sting persisting or dissipating. You get to decide how much (or how little) things are going to bother you. Every time you run into an obstacle, you have another opportunity to use the challenge as inspiration—something to learn from and/or something to motivate you! More often than not, criticism is about your work or behavior, not *about you as a person*.

Stay Focused on the Path Ahead.

Don't let criticism take you off course. It's tempting to go down the rabbit hole of rumination when you receive criticism—reading more into what was said than was there, making assumptions about the other person, even having imaginary arguments with them in your mind. What a time suck! Keep your eyes on the prize. When you focus on what you're trying to accomplish, criticism will bounce off you. For example, if you learned how to drive a car, at some point your instructor told you to "Look where you want to go." Or in sports, you're trained to "Look where you want the ball to go." The same goes for your aspirations. Keep your focus on your desired outcome, rather than on criticism, and you will achieve your goals.

CHAPTER 8

Twelve Tips for Saying "No" & Setting Boundaries

Boundaries don't protect you from other people. Boundaries protect you from you. It's really important for you to define for yourself what you will tolerate and what you won't.[31]
—Mel Robbins

I. Was. Exhausted. Not your run of the mill, had-a-lot-on-during-the-day exhausted; but the knocked-down, dragged-out kind of exhausted where my body was rebelling and I didn't have the energy or motivation to get out of bed. I'd done it again... taken on *way* too much, and *once more* I was thinking, "How the hell did I get here again?"

Sound familiar? This cycle of over-committing and burnout is common for people-pleasers. The more people I talk to, the more I see I am not alone! Almost everyone I've asked said they feel mild to extreme anxiety about needing to say "No," and/or felt some level of guilt after saying "No." Why is it so hard for us to turn someone down?

One of the most toxic traits of people-pleasers is the need to take care of everyone else. This looks like saying "Yes" to things when we want to say "No" and going along with things when we'd rather be doing something else.

See where the approval addiction and codependency come in? Hop

---

31 Mel Robbins, "The Mistake Everyone Makes with Boundaries," Mel Robbins Facebook Page, April 21, 2022, https://www.facebook.com/watch/?v=1085148852064464.

back to Chapter 3 if you need a little refresher on this concept. In order to break free of our approval addiction and codependent tendencies, it is crucial to learn to say "No" diplomatically, in a way that doesn't create loopholes. Here are some tips to assist you:

TWELVE TIPS FOR SAYING "NO" AND OVERCOMING THE FEAR OF CONFLICT

1. Realize you have a choice.

Look into your "Yes person" behavior. There's a script running through your mind that tells you, "I don't have any choice but to say "Yes." It's important to reprogram your mind, and remind yourself that you *do* have a choice, in every situation, and that includes the choice to say "No."

• Affirm to yourself right now: *I have a choice in all situations, and that includes saying "No."*

• To cement this statement into your psyche, repeat this affirmation to yourself multiple times a day, in the mirror if possible. Set a reminder on your phone with this affirmation for morning and night. After a while, you will notice that the way you handle life shifts and changes. Be patient with yourself, though. You didn't learn this behavior overnight, and it won't change overnight. But with consistency and persistence, any thought process can be changed.

2. Figure out your priorities and values.

One reason people-pleasers get so burnt out is because they're saying "Yes" to things that don't align with their priorities and values. Some don't even know what their priorities and values are! A lot of us have become so used to going along with what the people around us want, we've never stopped to consider what we want out of life. Take time out to explore this. You can write the answers to the questions below in a journal or right here in this book.

• What are your dreams for your life? (financial freedom, travel, inner peace, confidence, etc.)

_____

_____

_____

_____

_____

_____

• Which things/actions do you need to prioritize in order to reach these dreams? (speaking with a financial advisor, saving money, meditation, affirmations, etc.)

_____

_____

_____

_____

_____

_____

• What is really important to you? What do you value in life?

_____

_____

_____

_____

_____

_____

• Which things/actions do you need to prioritize in your life in order to stick to these values?

_____

_____

_____

_____

_____

_____

3. Reframe confrontation.

Disagreeing with someone doesn't mean that you're "fighting." It means that you are two unique adults with different opinions. It's not about blaming someone else or proving who's right or wrong in a situation. Working to resolve a conflict means that you are standing up for yourself and expressing your true feelings. It's important to let others know when we feel angry or frustrated and not to bottle those feelings up. Expressing your feelings at the moment will ensure problematic issues don't continue to happen. More often than not, people will respect your feelings and work with you to rectify the situation.

4. Using empathic assertion.

Empathic Assertion is the recognition of the other person's situation or feelings, followed by another statement standing up for your own rights.[32] Using this technique can help the other person feel seen while helping you to ask for what you need.

Examples of Empathic Assertion:

- "I know you're feeling angry and frustrated while you wait for a response. But the best I can do is give you a ballpark estimate of how long it will take."

- "I understand you're busy, and I am too, but it is difficult for me to finish this project on my own. So I want you to help me complete it."

- "I understand you're under a time constraint and I'd like to help, but I don't have the bandwidth to take on any other projects right now."

If you're used to saying "Yes" to everything all the time, using any kind of assertion might feel selfish, even mean. Being assertive and saying "No" does not make you a selfish or evil person. It makes you responsible. You are being responsible for yourself and your energy, which

---

[32] Melanie Newton, "How to Harness the Five Types of Assertion to Get Your Voice Heard," Business Business Business, accessed on Sept. 12, 2022, https://www.businessbusinessbusiness.com.au/harness-five-types-assertion-get-voice-heard/.

allows space for you to do a superb job on the projects you're working on and allows you to be more available for your loved ones. Think about it: Which version of you is your family and loved ones getting after you've been running around exhausting yourself for other people all day? Don't you want them to have the best of you? Don't you want *you* to have the best of you?

5. Resist the urge to over-explain.

When you assert yourself, it's inevitable that you will encounter the urge to over-explain why you are setting boundaries or turning someone down. The idea driving this behavior is that if you explain why you're saying "No," in great detail, this will soften the blow and spare the other person's feelings. See the people-pleasing and codependency sneaking in again? There are so many layers to this.

I know it's a cliche, but "No" is a complete sentence. You don't owe anyone an explanation for why you don't want to do something. It might feel like you do, but you don't. Just because you used to show up a certain way doesn't mean that you have to continue to show up that way. You can change. You can say "No." You can prioritize the things that are important to you over what someone else needs. That doesn't mean skirting responsibilities. I mean, you still have to feed your kids, but doing someone a favor that's going to take three hours when you're already stretched thin is not more important than your sanity.

You don't owe anyone an explanation.

Plus, when you over explain your situation, you open loopholes for the other person to corral you into saying "Yes" to the thing you're trying to decline. So just say "No" in whatever way feels comfortable, and leave it at that. *There are scripts at the end of this Chapter that will give you some loophole-free ways to say "No."*

6. Use a time delay to relieve stress.

This is one of my favorite techniques. We can get so used to saying "Yes" to everyone and everything that it can become a reflex. So rather than saying "Yes" right away, practice saying something like "Let me check my schedule and get back to you" or "I'll get back to you on this in twenty-four hours." This gives you breathing room to take stock of what you already have going on, to see if you have the capacity to add this to your plate, and to explore whether you want to do that thing. Cross-reference the item against the list of core values you made for yourself. If you decide you can't commit to the task or that it doesn't align with your values, you can use one of the "No" Scripts at the end of this Chapter to decline.

7. Set a time limit.

Have you ever said "Yes" to something, and then the project kept expanding? More and more tasks kept being added to your plate with no talk of additional compensation? The volunteer gig you thought was going to be a one-hour-a-week commitment grows to consume six hours a week? In project management, this is called "scope creep."

By definition, scope creep refers to "changes, [or] continuous or uncontrolled growth in a project's scope, at any point after the project begins. This can occur when a project is not defined, documented, or controlled. It is considered harmful."[33]

Did you catch that end part? Scope creep is considered *harmful*. I couldn't agree more! Having one project or responsibility growing beyond your means is stressful... but if multiple commitments get out of hand, it can lead to burnout and exhaustion! So how do we avoid scope creep in our lives? The best way is to have firm parameters and boundaries from the outset about the time you will commit to the task. If you're volunteering for something, say, up front, "I'm happy to help. Right now I can commit one hour per week to volunteer duties, and no more." In business, you can put it this way, "I estimate this project will take thirty hours to complete, which will cost $2,250.00. Any time spent beyond the thirty hours will be billed separately. I will keep in touch with you on my time spent as we go along to keep us on time and on budget." Be sure to set your time/commitment parameters up front to avoid confusion and manage expectations.

8. Manage expectations.

It's so important that we outline what we can do and can't/won't do, so

---

[33] "Scope Creep," Wikipedia, accessed August 15, 2022, https://en.wikipedia.org/wiki/Scope_creep.

there is no gray area, confusion, or exaggerated expectations.

I'll use an example from early in my design career. Back in the day, I was taking on whatever work came my way because I thought that that's how you "made it." I was hired to create a website for a client (I'll call her Kathy), which was within my wheelhouse. Once the website was completed, Kathy asked if I managed social media and would do this for her business. I said "Yes," resolving that I would learn as I went. Long story short, managing social media is not in my wheelhouse. I ended up doing a subpar job, not feeling inspired by the work, and wasn't able to grow Kathy's social media presence. She paid me her hard-earned money, wasn't satisfied with the service, and I was embarrassed because I had committed to something I couldn't deliver.... This created a lose-lose situation. I worked out a deal with Kathy that corrected this misstep and rebuilt her trust in me. But I could have avoided all of that mess if I'd said, "I'd like to help you with your social media, but that isn't in my wheelhouse. Can I help you find someone who does this professionally?" Then we both could have avoided disappointment and the subsequent ironing-out process.

It's important to manage expectations on both sides. Set yourself and the other person up for success by knowing what you can and can't do, and be clear about that when you commit to something.

9. Follow through with the boundaries you set.

This can be tricky for people-pleasers. You've built up the courage to say "No" and have done so politely. You think you're out of the woods. Time passes, and the other person circles back to say "I can't find anyone to do the thing you said you couldn't do." You feel pressured to help, even though you already said you can't. *Do not succumb to this internal pressure. You said "No" for a reason.* The compulsion to please can be strong— especially when it seems you are the only person who can save the day (our egos love being the superhero, by the way). This kind of situation is the genuine test of your boundaries and your resolve to take care of yourself first.

If you find yourself in this position, come back to the first few points in this Chapter:

- Realize you have a choice.

- Use empathic assertion to state your boundary again.

- Resist the urge to over-explain.

- Use a time delay to relieve stress.

- Use the "No" Scripts at the end of this Chapter to decline a second time.

I can't stress enough how important it is to follow through on the boundaries you set. This shows massive internal strength and reinforces for the people around you that you are showing up differently. If people around you have gotten used to you being the "Yes person" all the time, it's going to take repetition and consistency for them to realize that you are not living that way anymore. Every time you follow through on your boundaries, you reinforce for yourself and the people around you that you have self-respect and that you will only commit to things that will allow you to follow through.

10. Don't fear the fallout.

You may face resistance and/or fallout when you assert your boundaries and say "No." Human beings do not like change. Even if it's a good change, we resist it. So when you start changing, be prepared to meet resistance from the people around you. It's not because they necessarily have malicious intent; they just have an idea in their mind of who you are and how you show up. When you don't show up in that way, their minds don't know how to process this new information. Cue resistant assertions like, "This just isn't like you," "I've never seen this side of you," and "When did you become so selfish?" Though these statements may stir up the urge to explain yourself or defend the changes you are making, don't go there. When someone is in this resistant state, they are not in a place to hear you or be present with you.

If you're a people-pleaser, this situation can be challenging because you are facing your greatest fear: *standing face-to-face with someone who is not happy with you.* Take a deep breath. Remember, this is their resistance talking. You are not obligated to be at anyone's beck and call.

Standing in this truth can feel scary or unsettling. The first time I did this, I thought I was going to barf. But the longer I stood my ground, the more things calmed down. The more I practiced, the less unnerving it became. When you practice this, you will experience the same transformation. I promise.

11. Self-soothe.

There comes a time after asserting new boundaries and experiencing fall-out that you will experience a sense of loneliness. Your ego will try to convince you that no one will ever love this new version of you. This is your ego trying to keep you "safe" in the familiar, and get you back into people-pleasing mode. You must stay strong in these moments. Soothe your ego so you can continue moving forward in this new life direction. In the past, the way you soothed yourself was to get involved in other people's lives and make them feel better, which made you feel better. But you're not doing that now, so how do you soothe yourself through this discomfort?

- First, realize the value of *putting yourself first*. People-pleasers are used to putting themselves last and it can take convincing for them to believe they are worthy of giving themselves the same care they're doling out. You are more than worthy of the care you've been giving to others. In fact, you are way overdue. Let it in.

- Ground yourself with a repetitive task. Whether that's doing dishes or digging in the garden, running around the block or crocheting a blanket, doing repetitive tasks takes you out of panic mode and into a meditative flow state in which your nervous system calms down.

- Adopt a soothing word or phrase you can repeat to yourself whenever you feel anxiety arise. Here are some examples:

  › *I made the right decision for myself.*

  › *I am taking care of myself.*

  › *Peace, peace, peace.*

  › *Everything is going to be fine.*

• Stretch your body, gently, even for ten minutes. Focus all of your attention on breathing into your muscles. Feel them extending.

• Take a shower. Imagine the water pulling all the anxious energy off your body and washing it down the drain.

12. Realize you can't be everything to everyone.

This can be a hard pill to swallow, because many people-pleasers have gotten into what I call "superhero mode," and convinced themselves that without them, the entire world will fall apart (or at least be super dirty). Well, I've got news for you, my friend: *The world will keep turning even if you pull back. Those people will find someone else to support them if you can't.* Oof....I know.

> *The truth will set you free, but first it will piss you off.*[34]
>
> —Gloria Steinem

It's true. The world will not be knocked off its axis if you say "No." That's your mind speaking out of fear and resistance. Once you say "No" and take care of yourself and your energy, you will have time and enthusiasm for the important parts of your life, like date night with your spouse or playing with your kids or pets—because you won't be burnt out.

Going back to the topic of managing expectations, it's important to manage your expectations of *yourself.* After using the above techniques to make my life spacious, I sat down with my partner and said, "How did I do all those things before? How was I able to keep that pace?" He answered: "adrenaline." He was right. Without realizing it, I was in fight-or-flight mode, running on fumes. There wasn't time to stop, reflect, or often, even eat. I was stretched so thin that if for one moment, I had taken my eyes off the prize, the web of responsibilities and deadlines I had created would have devoured me. I was over-committed and over-stimulated. I had zero energy to connect with the people in my life who mattered the most. The things we get used to...it's weird.

---

[34] Gloria Steinem, *The Truth Will Set You Free, But First It Will Piss You Off!: Thoughts on Life, Love, and Rebellion* (New York: Random House, 2019).

Pretty much every people-pleaser I've connected with has this same cycle of overextension and adrenaline-fueled fury dictating their lives. It's important to recognize and stop this cycle before we end up burnt out, or worse, in the hospital, wishing we had more time for important things. Our time on this planet is finite. It's vital that we are intentional and create boundaries for how we extend ourselves.

*

LOOPHOLE-FREE WAYS TO SAY "NO"

As promised, here are some different "'No' Scripts" you can try as you practice having boundaries.

- "Thank you, but I'll have to pass on that." (Just say that, nothing more).

- "Thanks for considering me, but my calendar is booked up for the next few months. Can you circle back to me in (name the month)?"

- "I wish I could help you out, but I don't have the bandwidth to take on anything else right now."

- "Mary does that. I'll give you her contact info."

- "Thanks so much for the invite, but that's the day of my son's soccer game, and I never miss those."

- "Let me think about that, and I'll get back to you."

- "I'm not sure about my availability on that day. Let me check my calendar when I get home and circle back to you."

- "I'm sorry, but I'm maxed out right now and can't help with that."

- "I just don't have time right now. Let me recommend someone who might help."

- "I appreciate you asking me, but my time is already committed to other things."

- "I can't present at your event, but I can help you promote it on my social media/website!"

• "Sorry, but I'm already booked on that day."

• "I can't today, but I could help you on Friday morning between 9:00 to 10:00 a.m. if that works for you." (Note the specific time frame to avoid scope creep).

How to Say "No" After You've Said "Yes"

We've all been there! You agree to something and then get home and realize you've double booked yourself or don't have the time or energy to take this thing on. Here are a few ways that you can say "No" after you've already said "Yes":

• "I'm sorry. I know I said I would take on this project two months ago, but my situation has changed and I don't feel I'd be able to give your project my 100 percent. Let me suggest a couple of people who might help.

• "Apologies, but something has come up and I won't have the bandwidth to take this on after all. I wanted to let you know before the event so you could have time to fill my spot."

• "I know I committed last week to meeting up, but I'm just not feeling up to socializing right now. Can we please reschedule?"

• "I'm so sorry, but I said 'Yes' before looking at my calendar and then realized that I've double booked myself. Do you have other times that would work?"

CHAPTER 9

Radical Self Care

You are only free when you realize you belong no place—
you belong every place—no place at all. The price is high.
The reward is great.[35]

—Maya Angelou

Belonging was something I strived for—worked my ass off for—for decades. I could bend myself into the shape of any social container I entered and get along with many people, but I never felt like I belonged anywhere. I wondered if I would ever find "my place." It took much wandering and healing, deep exploration, and often-difficult reflection to realize that the place I belonged was in my heart. When I first ventured into the secret garden of my heart space, I didn't feel at home. It felt foreign. It was overgrown with thistles. There were brick walls and a labyrinth of pain and traumatic memories to navigate to the center—to my true home. Once I made it to the epicenter of myself, I breathed the deepest sigh of relief. *Finally.* All this time, I'd been searching outside myself, moving houses and towns, trying on personalities and fashions. The whole time, what I was looking for was the *home inside me.*

Getting to this place took serious elbow grease. Just as it takes time and effort to clear a chunk of property and build a thriving garden, it takes time and effort to clear the debris of our minds and spirits and make room to build new beds, add fresh soil with healthy compost, plant our new seeds, and watch them grow.

---

[35] Maya Angelou, interview by Bill Moyers, Moyers & Company, 1973.

SELF-LOVE

The term "self-love" has emerged in the online scene and has been paired with myriad definitions—with good reason, because self-love looks different for each of us. But what *is it*? According to the Brain and Behavior Research Foundation, "….Self-love is a state of appreciation for oneself that grows from actions that support our physical, psychological and spiritual growth."[36] Self-love is the opposite of people-pleasing—it's taking care of your own needs and not sacrificing your welfare to please others. This can be a slippery slope into self-absorbed territory, so the key is *balance*. Can you nourish your own soul, know your limits (and play within them), and serve others from your overflow?

Self-love can take many forms. What things make you feel supported? Hint: examine what you're seeking from other people. Give yourself *that*. Here are some examples of what self-love can look like:

- Speaking kindly to and about yourself.

- Prioritizing yourself and the things that matter to you.

- Setting healthy boundaries.

- Listening to your body and giving it what it needs.

- Listening to your intuition and trusting yourself.

- Standing up for yourself.

- Taking breaks from work to move and stretch.

- Putting your phone away and melting into the present moment.

- Forgiving yourself when you've been harsh with yourself.

Self-love is radical acceptance of yourself as you are. It's having compassion for yourself when you're moody, trusting yourself, keeping your word to yourself, and treating yourself as you would your best friend. When you practice self-love, you are becoming your own best friend. Think about your best friend (even if it's your dog). Think about how much you love them unconditionally and support them when they're

---

[36] Jeffrey Borenstein, M.D., "Self-Love and What It Means," Brain & Behavior, February 12, 2020, https://www.bbrfoundation.org/blog/self-love-and-what-it-means.

struggling. You'd do anything for them, right? What if they're down or moody? You don't shame them. You listen, hold space for them, and hold them close while they cry. You encourage them, cheer them up, and tell them how awesome they are. You remind them of their greatness when they forget.

In becoming your own best friend, you offer *yourself* this beautiful, loving treatment. You cultivate unconditional love for yourself and have compassion when you make mistakes or are moody. You hold yourself when you're down, encourage yourself, and hold space for whatever you're going through in the moment...just like you do with your best friend. Treating yourself with kindness melts away codependent tendencies. You give yourself everything you need, rather than seeking these things outside of yourself. You build a whole, balanced relationship *with yourself,* and balance out your external relationships.

PRACTICING RADICAL SELF-CARE

As we have seen, self-care is essential if you want to live a balanced life and give the best of yourself to the world. There's a lot of hype on the internet about taking bubble baths and eating chocolate cake, but deep, authentic self-care is about creating a safe place within your body for your spirit to live. It's learning to open up to receive the same love and care you give to others. It's learning to hold space for all your emotions... and for all of yourself. It's giving yourself the unconditional love you've been seeking outside of yourself. It's turning your attention inward and holding space for whatever you are feeling with compassion. It's re-parenting yourself.

RE-PARENTING YOURSELF

In "re-parenting yourself," you are taking on the role of a trustworthy, loving parent and creating a nurturing space within yourself where you can learn, grow, heal, and evolve. You are giving yourself structure and discipline in order to create new habits that will help you cope with tough situations, affirm yourself, and achieve the goals you've ignored for so long.

There are many ways to re-parent yourself and take back your power. All require self-discipline and consistency. As I put myself through this type of therapy, often I'd remark to close friends that "I feel like I'm re-learning how to do life!" And you are. You're teaching yourself new ways to *live*. Ones that will stick. Ones with longevity. Ones that, though they may seem rudimentary, will create lasting, positive changes in your life and leave you feeling empowered.

Change takes time. You're not going to overhaul your life overnight. Tackle things one at a time. Give yourself time to explore each aspect of your transformation—and nail it before you move on to the next one.

SELF-MIRRORING

Part of radical self-love is learning to mirror yourself. This practice will allow you to cultivate a safe, respectful relationship with yourself. So how do you do this? You've got to make space for your own thoughts and feelings and look at them from the perspective of a loving parent without judgment. Here are some ways you can do this:

Stream of Consciousness Writing Revisited

As you saw earlier, this intuitive writing style can be an effective tool. To reiterate, stream-of-consciousness writing (a "brain dump,") is where you sit down and write down every single thing that comes to mind, without stopping and without editing.

The way you can use this in self-mirroring is to start with the emotion that is coming up for you, and allow yourself to write down everything that comes to mind regarding that emotion. To best practice stream-of-consciousness writing, allow yourself time, at least fifteen minutes, where you will not be disturbed. Set a timer on your phone so your mind can focus on the task at hand, and don't look away from your paper or computer screen while you're writing. Don't worry about spelling or grammar. Resist the urge to edit, read or judge your writing. You're not writing a dissertation; you're processing your emotions.

Write until your timer runs out—then you can read it if you choose. You'll find that as you're writing, you'll receive insights into what you're experiencing. You may also experience waves of emotion and even feel the need to cry. Allow the tears to come; allow the emotions to flow. Keep writing.

Keep letting it out. This is how you heal.

Your mind might jump all over the place. Just keep writing. The more you follow your stream of consciousness, the more you will see all the thoughts link and flow. You can follow the stream deep into the heart of your emotion, down to the core wound. Once you get there, hold yourself with gentleness. Be with the emotion. Express the emotion that comes up. Resist the urge to judge anything. More often than not, at the base of every powerful emotion is a wound your inner child carries. Seeing this from an Observer point of view allows you to mirror yourself in the way you needed to be mirrored when you were growing up.

How do you mirror yourself *after* an exercise like this? By acknowledging the validity of your own feelings. This might look like saying out loud (or in your head), "In this writing, I see your feelings of frustration and betrayal. Your feelings are valid and you have every right to feel them." It doesn't need to be much more than that. Just acknowledging your own emotions and validating them can bring about a profound healing response.

SELF-VALIDATION

When we're deep in people-pleasing behavior, we're looking for validation from the people around us. This is the main reason we become people-pleasers—to please others so they will approve of us and validate our worth. So if we wish to flip the script and be our own safe space, we've got to learn ways to validate ourselves. Following are some examples of ways to do this:

Mirror Work and Affirmations

They say the eyes are the window into the soul. When was the last time you gazed into your own eyes? What's your relationship with your mirror like? Have you thought about it? Have you noticed what you do when you get in front of a mirror? What do you say to yourself? Which parts of your body do you notice first and what do you say about your body in your head? Do you dread looking in the mirror?

Mirror Work is a powerful practice that was popularized by transformational teacher and self-love expert Louise Hay, who authored numerous self-help books including *Heal Your Body: The Mental Causes for Physical Illness and the Metaphysical Way to Overcome Them*,[37] and *Mirror Work: 21 Days to Heal Your Life*.[38] In the latter book, Louise says that Mirror Work is the most effective way she's found for learning to love yourself and see the world as a safe and loving place. Her book on the subject says that you will become more aware of the words you say and the things you do after practicing Mirror Work consistently – which will teach you how to take care of yourself on a deeper level than you have done before.

Mirror Work is strange, sometimes uncomfortable, embarrassing at first, and ultimately healing. It's a portal into the depths of your soul, where you can meet with your inner child and reconnect with the long-lost parts of yourself. The first time I sat down to try Mirror Work, I could barely look at myself. It was awkward. After I'd held my gaze for over fifteen seconds, I bawled my eyes out. I wanted to move away from the mirror and distract myself with something…anything…but I knew I had to stay and *do the work*. After staring at myself for a while, the wave of shame passed, and I felt a connection with my soul. I'd never felt anything like it. I stumbled through speaking the affirmations to myself, not believing them at first. I committed to practicing Mirror Work for fifteen minutes each morning before I got into my morning routine. This practice changed my life on many levels. I became more confident in myself, my beauty, and my power. I asserted myself at work and in my personal life, began attracting more opportunities to make an income, and even lost weight (even though I kept my diet and exercise regimen the same!). I think what melted off me was emotional baggage from the shame I'd been feeling for so many years. The stranger part? My face changed. As I continued with my Mirror Work and other parts of my healing journey, a maturity and glow came over my face. If you look at pictures of me from 7 years ago, I look like a different person! I recommend Mirror

---

[37] Louise Hay, *Heal Your Body: The Mental Causes for Physical illness and the Metaphysical Way to Overcome Them* (Hay House Inc., Jan. 1, 1984).
[38] Louise Hay, *Mirror Work: 21 Days to Heal Your Life* (Hay House Inc., March 22, 2016).

Work to anyone I speak to about self-worth and confidence, because it's a game-changer.

If you're interested in doing a deep dive into this work, check out Louise Hay's book. For now, I'll give you a quick explanation of Mirror Work and tips to make your practice effective. To practice Mirror Work, sit or stand in front of a mirror for at least five minutes, holding your own gaze as you speak affirmations to yourself.

Five Tips for Practicing Mirror Work

1. Practice in private so you aren't disturbed. Sometimes emotions can surface and it's best to have the space to allow whatever surfaces to be processed without interruption.

2. Use affirmations that feel authentic. If you use affirmations that don't feel authentic, it will create a dissonance in your mind.

3. Commit to yourself. Dedicate at least five minutes per day to connect with yourself. If you're concerned about losing track of time, set a timer.

4. Be gentle with yourself if you feel emotional during this process. Allow yourself space to feel whatever emotions arise.

5. Keep a journal while you practice Mirror Work. Record notable experiences. It's interesting to look back and see how much healing has happened and how far you've come!

Celebrate Your Mini-Victories

It can be easy to plow through your day and get to the end, wondering where the time went. Did you accomplish anything? One way to recognize your efforts and validate your hard work is to take time at the end of each day to write three mini-victories you had—and celebrate them. It might seem trivial, but looking back over your mini-victories will paint a new picture for yourself of your productivity and your worth.

Ten mini-victories you can celebrate:

1. Writing that blog post you've been thinking of doing forever.

2. Getting a haircut after weeks of putting it off.

3. Writing out post-dated cheques to pay off a debt.

4. Making a breakthrough with your child.

5. Having a cool bonding moment with your spouse.

6. Building that planter box you wanted.

7. Reading a Chapter of an inspirational book instead of watching Netflix.

8. Allowing yourself time to relax when you needed it.

9. Standing up for yourself.

10. Setting boundaries and keeping them.

Every bit of progress you make each day adds up to significant changes and ultimate success! Nine times out of ten, any "overnight success" is the culmination of many years of dedicated and persistent work. You've got this! Bonus points if you celebrate yourself in front of a mirror.

SELF-SOOTHING

We're going to run into situations that are difficult or that trigger a strong emotional reaction inside of us sometimes. Self-soothing gives us space to feel our emotions and take care of ourselves during life's trials and tribulations. Find self-soothing techniques that resonate for you and that make you feel good and comforted. If this is all unfamiliar territory, try out a bunch of different things to figure out what works for you.

Here are some examples of ways you can self-soothe:

- Close your eyes for a while.
- Dim the lights and light some candles.
- Doodle fluid, abstract shapes and forms.
- Drink something warm.
- Give yourself a hand or foot massage.
- Go for a walk in nature.

• Let yourself cry if you feel it coming on.

• Place your hands over your heart and feel it beating. Close your eyes and focus there for a few minutes.

• Put on calming meditation music.

• Put on some aromatherapy or burn some incense.

• Put on comfy clothes.

• Stand up and shake your body for thirty seconds.

• Starting with your face, contract and relax all the muscles in your body, all the way down to your toes.

• Stretch your body, holding each stretch for thirty seconds.

• Take a warm shower or a long bath.

• Try some breathing exercises—go back to the 4x4 Breath and Straw Breath in Chapter 5.

• Try mindfulness in the moment—focus on one noise, smell, or sensation around you.

• Try a guided meditation track.

• Visualize a calm place or a happy memory.

• Wrap your arms around yourself and give yourself a thirty-second hug.

• Wrap yourself in layers of blankets or try a weighted blanket.

SELF-DISCIPLINE

Disciplining yourself might not come to mind when you think of self-love, but self-discipline is keeping your promises to yourself. Some of the deepest pain people-pleasers feel is that of losing time—watching precious hours in which you could be building your dreams or looking after yourself slip away as you vanish into the vortex of everyone else's needs. Days turn into weeks, weeks into months, and months into years as your life slips between your fingers. Before you know it, decades have passed and you *still* haven't done that thing for yourself you wanted to do. It sucks. It hurts because you haven't made *yourself* a priority. Deep down, you know you could have. You lose trust in yourself, because you failed to keep your word to yourself.

A huge act of self-love is keeping your own promises—showing up for yourself in the way you wish others would have shown up for you. Learning to hold yourself accountable for *your own goals* is empowering, and it can help to calm your nervous system, because you are creating a safe place *within yourself* for your own dreams and desires. You are *seeing and mirroring* yourself in a healthy way.

This could look a few different ways:

1. Take time to *figure out your own goals. Write them down.* After people-pleasing for so long, you might not even know what you want from life anymore. Give yourself time and space to explore the dreams you had put aside. Break down what it would take to achieve them. It doesn't matter if they seem silly to your logical brain. Allow your inner child to come out and play!

2. Schedule time every morning, before you get into your day, to meditate, read something uplifting, or practice something that enriches your spirit. Even five minutes can make a tremendous difference in your life.

3. Make time every day to get some type of exercise, whether it's hitting the gym or getting your steps out in nature.

4. Grab a calendar or download an app and plan out your month with all of the action steps you are going to take toward your goals. Cross them off when you complete them.

5. Block out times in your daily calendar for all the things that are important to you. When you sit down and block out the time it takes to do everything you need to do in a day, you'll be amazed at how much time everything actually takes. Doing this helps you to visualize your day and the time you have available for extras. Whenever someone asks you to do something for them, look at your calendar. Do you have space for it? Create the habit of prioritizing your own goals, and don't move or give up your own blocks unless it's important.

6. Be diligent with your financial decisions. Create a plan to get you to your goals. Start at the end and reverse-engineer the process. Then, before you buy something, ask yourself, "Is this going to contribute to my financial goals or take away from them?"

These are just a few ideas to get you started. There are many other ways you can practice self-discipline. A simple Google search will bring you a myriad of options. Pick one item and focus on it with all of your energy for at least twenty-one days. Doing so consistently for that amount of time will start to create new neural pathways in your brain and create new habits. Sometimes it takes longer for things to stick. Practice one item until it feels like second nature, then move on to the next thing. You will find your own groove.

*

THE ACCOUNTABILITY DETOX

Alright, it's time to sit down and let yourself off the hook. Call all of your energy back from all the people you're thinking about, worrying about, and feel you need to save. Free yourself from the pressure to do more, be more, work late, and extend yourself further. Allow yourself to just…

be.

here.

now.

Take a deep breath into your belly, relax your shoulders, and sink into the surface that is holding you right now.

You are enough.
You are doing enough.
You have done enough.
You have given enough.
You don't need to prove your worth to anyone.
You can allow yourself to be free.
Exhale. Allow this to sink in.
It's not your job to save anyone.
It's not your job to make others happy.
You are not responsible for the emotional reactions of others.
You do not have to change yourself to appease anyone.
You are perfectly worthy *as you are.*
You do not have to earn love and support.
It's safe to receive.
It's safe to let others help you.
It's safe to soften.
It's okay to pull back.
It's okay to look after yourself.

Allow the pressure to release from your body, and allow your nervous system to relax and recalibrate.

What would your life be like if you weren't pulled in a million directions?

What would it be like if you allowed yourself to be nourished?

What would it feel like if you didn't have all the pressure to be everything to everyone?

This is what we're getting into with the Accountability Detox. If you've read this book this far, it's likely that you've assumed the responsibility for myriad other people's emotional state and happiness level. You've given your all to others and wondered, "Is it enough?" You've felt an overwhelming *need* to be of service, to help, even to save others. But this is not your job. And that *need* is part of the codependent pull to become entangled with others. It's time to untangle yourself and be free.

Examine the relationships in your life. Ask yourself...

• Where am I overextending myself or feeling responsible for others?

_____

_____

_____

_____

_____

_____

• Am I enabling my friend to stay in a toxic cycle because I'm afraid to speak my truth?

_____

_____

_____

_____

_____

• Do I allow others to disrespect me because I don't want to rock the boat?

_____

_____

_____

_____

_____

_____

• Do I feel taken advantage of by someone but say nothing?

_____

_____

_____

_____

_____

_____

These dynamics can be shifted by making different choices. It might not always feel great, but choosing yourself and your wellbeing is how you take your power back. This is another way to have boundaries—to establish for yourself where you end and others begin, and to hold fast to those boundaries in your daily interactions until your relationships balance out. Here are some examples:

1. Telling your peer you don't appreciate being disrespected in your own home and won't tolerate that kind of treatment anymore—remembering that you have just as much right to speak your mind as they do, and you don't have to continue to be mistreated just to keep a friend around.

2. Telling your relative that as much as you love seeing them, you'd appreciate it if they called ahead and made plans instead of showing up unannounced. You can set the terms of how others enter your space.

3. Explaining to your superior at work that the additions to your workload are overwhelming you. Let them know if you're having a hard time keeping up or taking work home with you, and that you can't continue like this. Ask them to delegate some of the work to someone else or to hire more help. Remind them that you are one person with only so much energy, and that you need down time after work.

Choose one situation in your life in which you feel overextended or responsible, and work out a way to approach it differently. Maybe you have to have a conversation. Maybe you need to modify your expectations of yourself. As you make adjustments to your life, you will experience the phenomenon I've lovingly coined "The Accountability Detox." Over time, you notice that you become more relaxed and empowered, and create more time for yourself. As this happens, that *need to* please and help will vanish. You will help others because you *want to* and you have the space to. It's a different dynamic; a different energy exchange. Rather than serving others from a depleted or resentful place, you serve others from your overflow—pouring more love and peace into others, which the universe will reciprocate. You create a new reality for yourself and for the people around you. That's a beautiful thing.

CHAPTER 10

Rebuilding Your Life
Body, Mind & Spirit

I have already lost touch with a couple of people I used to be.[39]

—Joan Didion

The time has come to say goodbye. Goodbye to the old version of yourself, who cannot accompany you where you're going. In working through this book, you will have encountered beliefs, behaviors, and relationship dynamics you would like to shift. This is not simple work! Kudos to you for making it this far.

To move forward into the life you desire, it's important to honor the person you've been up to this point and release them so you can embark on a new journey into the unknown.

"But if I release my identity, what will be left?"

Your true and divine essence, that's what. The core of your soul transcends your personality, your memories, and all your thoughts about who you are. It takes courage to shed your old self, because you don't know yet who you will become. You venture into uncharted territory without a map, with faith that you'll end up where you're meant to be. Trust me—you will be glad you embarked on this quest. As long as you are heading toward authenticity, you are headed in the right direction. There is no

---

[39] Joan Didion, "Quotable Quote," Good Reads, Accessed July 9, 2022, https://www.goodreads.com/quotes/7330826-i-have-already-lost-touch-with-a-couple-of-people.

way you can get this wrong.

So, how do you let go of your old self? *Slowly.* Every time you release a belief or a habit, you replace it with a new, more supportive belief or habit. The most powerful changes we make in our lives happen when we change our routines. You must *practice* being a person who respects yourself, stands up for yourself, has boundaries, and says "No." At first it will feel uncomfortable…maybe even scary! You will face the pain of sacrificing the familiar in favor of the new. You might be tempted to go back to old ways.

But the more you practice, the more confident you will become, and the more you will develop the *habits* of being the new you! Just as you'd train to run a marathon, you must embrace the idea of *training* as the way to help you construct an empowering, fulfilling life. Success in anything requires consistency and dedication. Your accumulated changed behaviors will culminate into a new experience of life.

Training is something you have to do yourself. There's no one out there who can exercise for you or eat the right foods for you. *You have to do the work.* The same goes for training yourself to change your mindset. But oooh, is it ever satisfying when you see results. And the results will vary—from massive to minute. Sometimes you might not even notice the effects of your training until you're in a situation that used to rattle you and you notice, "I don't feel bothered." Won't that be amazing?

We are complex beings. It's important to address all the different aspects of our beings so we can create a balanced life. In this Chapter, we'll go over ways you can train your body, mind, and spirit to become healthier, stronger, and more resilient.

When you bring balance to one aspect of your life, you will naturally balance other areas. Something as simple as nourishing your body could provide a new sense of safety and stability for you, which could tell your body that it's safe to release pent up trauma and emotions. This might come out as tears, body quakes, even repressed memories surfacing to be witnessed. I encourage you to be *present with yourself* during experiences like these and to treat yourself with compassion. These "healing eruptions" are a necessary part of the process of your evolution.

Remember, you are the gatekeeper of your life. You get to decide what comes in and what doesn't. As you rebuild, allow your intuition to guide you. In the beginning, check in with yourself often. What resonates for you? What doesn't? In the rest of this Chapter, I'm going to discuss ways you can rebuild your life by improving aspects of Body, Mind and Spirit.

BODY

The body is your temple. Keep it pure and clean for the soul to reside in.[40]

—B.K.S. Iyengar

One of the most important aspects of healing from people-pleasing behavior is *getting back into your body.* When you are stuck in a pattern of pleasing others, you are disconnected from your body, your emotions, and your intuition. When you prioritize taking care of yourself, and bring your focus inward, that can feel overwhelming. So often people I work with say (and I have experienced this, too) that they are afraid to go inside of themselves. They're worried about what they might find. The crux is that if you want to heal for good, that's where you're going... into the depths of your being, your memories, your emotions, and your spirit.

So let's begin with learning how to fuel the physical body. Remember what I mentioned about *relearning how to do life?* You've got to start from the ground up, and it would amaze you how much healing can happen when you begin to look after your physical vessel. It's time to look after your body and your health. You only get one body, your health is your most precious commodity, and in order to give of yourself in a balanced way, you need to be healthy.

If you've been entrenched in people-pleasing for several years, chances are your adrenal system is shot. You haven't been getting adequate sleep, and you've either been overeating or under-eating to cope with stress. Be gentle with yourself as you assess where your body is at, and as you move through your healing process. As you start to care for your body, you may get emotional. You may experience days where you slip up and fall off a new routine or don't even want to get out of bed. This

---

[40] Kristin Russel, "Yoga Quotes of B.K.S. Iyengar," July 21, 2015, https://masteringyoga.org/yoga-quotes-of-b-k-s-iyengar-the-body-is-your-temple-keep-it/.

is all normal. Please be kind to yourself. Remind yourself that everyone makes mistakes—*and get yourself back on the horse!*

Now for a personal share...

There was a good year and a half in my healing process where every time I exercised; I would start crying. Sometimes I would have to get off the treadmill and bawl my eyes out for a while. Repressed memories came up, but sometimes nothing entered my conscious mind to be witnessed... my body just needed to release some energy. I want to share this with you, because as you prioritize yourself and take care of yourself, you may be overcome by enormous waves of emotion that sometimes seem like they come out of nowhere. Don't let this deter you from moving forward in your healing work.

In order to have a unique experience of life, we've got to do different things. So where do we start?

Get adequate sleep.

Have you heard of a sleep deficit? It's the difference between the amount of sleep a person needs and the sleep they're getting. Also known as "sleep debt," it racks up every time you don't sleep well. Sleep deprivation can cause a variety of issues, from irritability to memory loss, impaired moral judgment, hallucinations, and aches and pains. It can even increase your risk of heart disease and Type 2 diabetes. If that's not enough reason to get your butt to bed at a decent time, I don't know what is.

Sleep requirements are different for everyone, but a wonderful goal to strive for is seven to eight hours of sleep per night. If it's just not possible for you, make time for little cat naps during the day to help you catch up.

If you have trouble falling asleep, following are things you can do to help you wind down at the end of the day.

1. Stop using screens at least an hour before bedtime.
The screens on our phones, tablets, computers, and televisions emit a short-wavelength blue light similar to sunlight. Not only does this light make us more alert, it tricks the body into thinking it's daytime. This stops the production of melatonin, a hormone released by the pineal gland at night when there is

little to no light, to signal the body to prepare for sleep. Blue light exposure can end up pushing our bedtimes later and later, and lead to less restful sleep.

2. Stick to a sleep schedule.

Going to bed and getting up at the same time every day will help balance your circadian rhythm, which will help balance out myriad hormones in your body and contribute to other areas of your health. A regular sleep schedule calms your nervous system, and as your nervous system calms, stress-induced cortisol in your system diminishes. (This can even lead to weight loss). As you heal your sleep pattern, you become more focused and productive in your daily tasks as well.

3. Pay attention to what you eat and drink.

Don't go to bed hungry or stuffed—both disrupt your sleep. Try to avoid heavy meals a couple of hours before bedtime. Also, be cognizant of your consumption of nicotine, caffeine, and alcohol. Nicotine and caffeine are stimulants whose effects can take hours to wear off, and while alcohol might make you feel sleepy, it can disrupt your sleep if you consume it too late in the evening.

4. Create a restful environment.

An ideal environment to sleep in is cool, dark, and quiet. It's best not to keep phones or other light-emitting screens in your bedroom. If you keep your phone in your room, be sure to turn off the notifications and put it screen-down on your bed-side table so that the light from nighttime alerts doesn't disturb you. Consider using blackout shades, earplugs, a fan or white/brown noise machine, or other items to create your ideal environment. Do calming activities before bedtime, such as meditation, stretching, taking a bath, reading, etc. It's helpful to get into a bedtime routine, so your body gets to know that, for instance, after a long, hot bath, we're going to get ready for bed. After a while, your body will associate the bath with bedtime and will release melatonin while you're in the tub. Aren't our bodies amazing?

5. Limit daytime naps.

If you nap during the day, limit your naps to thirty minutes, as longer naps can interrupt nighttime sleep. If you work nights, however, you might need to nap late in the day before work to help make up your sleep debt.

*

Move your body every day.

In order for your body to fully assimilate vitamins, minerals, food, and water, you must move your body. Without exercise, there's little assimilation, and proper elimi-nation cannot take place.[41]

—Michael Bernard Beckwith, *Spiritual Liberation*

You don't have to be in the gym every day to move your body. Simple activities like walking or Tai Chi have amazing effects on the nervous system. You can dance, swim, bike, paddle board, ski, snowshoe, practice yoga asanas, play with your pets, or do some gardening…whatever you like! Moving your body activates your lymphatic system, which boosts your immune system and creates dopamine, the "happy hormone." Plus, you get that awesome feeling of satisfaction at the end of the day, know-ing that you worked your body. As a bonus, having had exercise during the day contributes to better sleep. According to family physician and researcher Dr. Wayne Jonas,

Exercise also improves cognition, mood, emotional regulation, and motor function. The Mayo Clinic (among other organiza-tions) supports the use of exercise for symptom management among those with depression.[42]

If you're already feeling burnt out or exhausted, the thought of add-ing more activity to your day might seem crazy. Physical activity is a pow-erful energizer, though. Start small, promising yourself a quick, five-min-

---

[41] Michael Bernard Beckwith, *Spiritual Liberation: Fulfilling Your Soul's Potential* (Atria Books/ Beyond Words, Nov. 8, 2008).

[42] Wayne Jonas, M.D., "Use Exercise to Increase Your Body's Ability to Heal," Psychology Today, Dec. 30, 2019, https://www.psychologytoday.com/ca/blog/how-healing-works/201912/use-exer-cise-increase-your-body-s-ability-heal.

ute walk or 1,000 more steps on your pedometer. Once you get out there, you will feel like doing more.

It's important to think of physical activity as a priority instead of something that can be postponed. Just like you make time to brush your teeth and shower each day, you've got to make time to move your body. Call it your *internal hygiene.* Getting daily movement will give your organs a "shower" to process energy, move lymphatic fluid, and encourage your body's processes of removing waste and producing more energy. You can also add a 30 second cold shower to your daily routine to encourage lymphatic flow.

You can start with slow, low-impact exercises like walking and work your way up. Many people start off intensely and hurt themselves. Be gentle with yourself while you are exercising. Start with activities your body can handle. Avoid movements that cause sharp pain. Check in with your body. Achy muscles are normal, but you want to avoid pain in the joints. If you're not sure where to start, consult your doctor or consider working with a trainer to assess where you're at. Build a plan. You've got this!

Hydrate.

I know, I know, you're thinking, "Okay, Mom!" But listen…up to sixty percent of the adult human body is water. In order for all your organs to function properly, you need to hydrate your body. Being dehydrated can make you feel fatigued, irritable, dizzy, and/or confused. When you're in that state, you won't make good decisions. So drink your water, please. There is a lot of different advice out there about how much water to consume.

> *The truth is, there is no magic formula for hydration — everyone's needs vary depending on their age, weight, level of physical activity, general health and even the climate they live in.*[43]

According to Chinese medicine, we eat when we are hungry and drink when we are thirsty, and only in amounts enough to match our physical needs. Consuming more than that would be going against nature and

---

[43] Brandon Specktor, "How Much WAter Do You Really Need to Drink?," Live Science, last updated Oct. 6, 2022, https://www.livescience.com/61353-how-much-water-you-really-need-drink.html.

cause ill health.

Though drinking water is important, hydration is not limited to water intake. Many foods and beverages we consume also contain water. Electrolytes are also important for your body to retain the water you take in and for proper brain and muscle function. Electrolytes are chemicals that conduct electricity when dissolved in water. Muscles and neurons are sometimes referred to as the "electric tissues" of the body. They rely on the movement of electrolytes through the fluid inside, outside, or between cells. So, to create optimal mental and physical functionality in the body, we need to have the proper balance of water *and* electrolytes.

Electrolytes in human bodies include:

- sodium,
- potassium,
- calcium,
- bicarbonate,
- magnesium,
- chloride, and
- phosphate.

One interesting pearl of wisdom I came across while learning about how my body works is that prolonged stress can skew your electrolyte balance. When I was stressed for a long period, I got to where I was tired all the time and craving salt. I couldn't figure out why this was happening. Then I happened across a video by scientist and lecturer Tracy Harrison from the School of Applied Functional Medicine called "Skewed Electrolyte Balance: A Purposeful Stress Response"[44] that explained how our body will throw our electrolytes out of balance in order to help us survive. I did not know that being stressed all the time was putting my body into survival mode and wreaking havoc on a plethora of bodily functions. Check out Dr. Harrison's video (and the rest of her work, if it resonates with you).

So, what can we consume to balance our electrolytes and stay hydrated? There are many electrolyte drinks and powders out there. You'll want

---

[44] Tracy Harrison, "Surprising Interconnectedness: Functional Medicine Insights on Complex Issues," The School of Applied Functional Medicine, July 13 2018, https://schoolafm.com/ws_clinical_know/functional-medicine-insights-on-complex-issues/.

to consume more electrolytes if you do a lot of exercise or are in a sauna or hot tub often. Don't overdo it, as there is such a thing as "too much of a good thing." If you want to do your own sleuthing, there are a lot of resources on the internet that lay out the different kinds of food that are rich in each of the electrolytes listed above.

Get an Assessment and/or Bloodwork Done.

Just like you get the oil changed in your car, it's important to keep up with preventative maintenance on your body. Though they're not always comfortable, getting regular check-ups can put your mind at ease or catch things before they grow into enormous problems. A doctor or naturopath will see where you're at hormonally, if you have any nutritional deficiencies, and if there is anything else you should know about. Your bloodwork can show you if your electrolytes are out of balance, among many other key health indicators. Sometimes a dentist or even an optometrist will see a disorder before a doctor can.

One day, having been deep in people-pleasing for decades, I realized I hadn't been to a dentist in over ten years! I was ashamed, and felt like I was a failure who couldn't even look after myself. I put off going for another few months because I was afraid the dentist would judge me as harshly as I'd been judging myself. When I got in there and got a cleaning and a filling, it was as if a massive weight fell off of me. The shame and worry melted away. I got into my car and teared up. I'd made an enormous deal out of such a small thing. I know many people avoid doing these not-so-sexy things for themselves. When you bite the bullet and allow yourself to be taken care of on a fundamental level, deep healing happens. Plus, getting a check-up will let you know where you're at and what you can adjust to get your body working optimally. You deserve that.

Put Good Food and Vitamins into Your Body.

Our soil and our food are not the same as they were 100 years ago. Much of our food is devoid of the proper nutrition we need, so it's important to supplement with good quality vitamins and minerals. If you're on a tight budget, a good all-purpose multivitamin will help. If you want to up the ante, get a good quality, non-GMO, organic green powder into your routine. This will give you amazing nutrition without you having to get creative with salads every day. My favorite is Greens+ Multivitamin powder. I'm not affiliated with the company; I just take it every day—and feel amazing because of it. There are so many out there to choose from these days. Grab one that gives you a broad range of vitamins and minerals. You can mix it into a smoothie or mix in some juice or water and down it. (Check the labels to make sure that you're not allergic to any of the ingredients.)

As I mentioned, minerals are important to help us stay hydrated. Some minerals are essential for absorbing certain vitamins, and vice versa. Ask your local pharmacist or naturopath for recommendations and try out different things until you find what makes your body feel lovely.

Heal Your Gut.

There is a strong connection between the health of your gut and the health of your mind and emotions. In the new field of Nutritional Psychiatry, doctors help patients understand how gut health and diet can affect their mood positively or negatively. There is anatomical and physiological two-way communication between the gut and brain via the vagus nerve. The gut-brain axis offers us a greater understanding of the connection between diet and disease, including depression and anxiety.

One study[45] shows that deficiencies in long-chain Omega-3 fatty acids, B-vitamins, zinc, magnesium, and vitamin D can cause depressive symptoms, and supplemental forms of these nutrients are used in clinical treatment of mild-to-moderate symptoms. We are just beginning to understand the use of food as medicine in North American society. In developed countries, we are eating more sugar and processed foods than ever before, which can cause myriad health issues and subsequent mood and behavioral issues.

While consuming more whole foods and supplements can affect our mental health, we can't look to dietary changes to cure mental health challenges…just like you can't exercise your way out of a poor diet. As I mentioned earlier, we need a holistic approach to our wellness. Now that we've explored ways to bring our bodies back into balance, let's discuss ways we can improve mental health.

---

[45] Laura R LaChance and Drew Ramsey, "Antidepressant Foods: An Evidence-Based Nutrient Profiling System For Depression," National Library of Medicine, Sept. 20, 2018, https://www.ncbi.nlm.nih.gov/pmc/articles/PMC6147775.

*

MIND

*What we are today comes from our thoughts of yesterday,
and our present thoughts build our life of tomorrow: Our
life is the creation of our mind.*

—Siddhārtha Gautama

I'm glad we are talking more about mental health these days. Mental health includes our emotional, psychological, and social well-being. It affects how we think, feel, and act, and helps determine how we handle stress, relate to others, and make choices. When we are healthy mentally, we enjoy life and the people in it. We can handle challenges, think clearly, are creative, and are apt to try new things, learn something new, and take risks.

Your mental health will ebb and flow as you experience different life events. Some things we go through in life can be traumatic and leave us feeling out of sorts. Other life events are subtle, but their effects can creep up on us. Before we know it, we're isolating ourselves and feeling off.

If you are struggling with mental health issues, please know that you are not alone. Mental health problems are common and can be treated. If you're not sure if you're dealing with a mental health problem, check the list below. Experiencing one or more of the following feelings or behaviors can be an early warning sign of a problem:

- Eating or sleeping too much or too little.
- Pulling away from people and usual activities.
- Having low or no energy.
- Feeling numb or like nothing matters.
- Having unexplained aches and pains.
- Feeling helpless or hopeless.
- Smoking, drinking, or using drugs more than usual.
- Feeling confused, forgetful, on edge, angry, upset, worried, or scared.
- Yelling or fighting with family and friends.
- Experiencing severe mood swings that cause problems in re-

lationships.
- Having persistent thoughts and memories you can't get out of your head.
- Hearing voices or believing things that are not true.
- Thinking of harming yourself or others.
- Inability to perform daily tasks like taking care of your kids or getting to work or school.

If you're struggling with your mental health, the best thing you can do is reach out to someone. Connection is the antidote to most mental health issues. Whether you reach out to a friend, coach, or counselor, talking things out can be cathartic and helpful. There is a list of resources at the end of this book that you can tap into if you're going through mental health challenges. If you don't feel you have anyone to talk to, I've added a list of hotlines you can call to talk to someone right away. You are never alone. This too shall pass, as the adage goes. To quote American author and entrepreneur Marie Forleo, "everything is figure-out-able."

The Mind-Body Connection

Mental health is also important because it can have a direct effect on your physical health. There are multiple published scientific studies that prove this link. If you follow the work of author Dr. Joe Dispenza or study the "placebo effect," you see that there is a definite link between our mind and our body. We can make ourselves sick from stress and toxic thoughts. On the flip side, though, we can also make ourselves well with an attitude of gratitude and positive thoughts.

If we can consciously tap into the autonomic nervous system, we can begin to influence the way our body functions physiologically.[46]

—Dr. Joe Dispenza, *The Role of Brainwaves in Meditation: Part 1*

How to Look After Your Mental Health

Here are some effective ways I've found to care for your mental health

---

[46] Joe Dispenza, "The Role of Brainwaves in Meditation: Part I," Unlimited Joe Dispenza, Dec. 12, 2020, https://drjoedispenza.com/blogs/dr-joes-blog/the-role-of-brainwaves-in-meditation-part-i.

and heal:

1. Reach out and ask for help.

It may be hard to admit that you need help or desire connection, but that first move will change everything and open you up to new opportunities to heal your mental health. Reaching out for support shows your sub-conscious mind and your body that it is safe to be vulnerable and allow others to help you.

2. Surround yourself with positive people.

We influence each other on so many levels. Look at the people you spend most of your time with.

- Are they positive?
- Are they doing things you want to be doing?
- Do you enjoy their company?
- Do they add value to your life?
- Do they inspire you?
- Do they hold you accountable?
- Do they encourage you?
- Do you feel happy and connected after spending time with them?

OR

- Are you hanging out with them out of a sense of obligation?
- Are they stuck in perpetual toxic cycles?
- Do they complain a lot?
- Do they have a lot of drama going on?
- Do they discourage your ideas?
- Do you feel drained, sad, anxious, or confused after spending time with them?
- Do they display the traits of a toxic person that we outlined in Chapter 4?

The most important part of our mental health is the environment we inhabit in our daily lives. Being in a calm environment with healthy people will do more for you than any magical green juice. If you're not in a position to change your external environment, use the following tips to change your internal environment.

3. Stop comparing yourself to other people.

Comparison is the thief of joy. Comparison is a time suck, and at worst, a toxic habit that can wreak havoc on your self-esteem. In this age of social media, it's even easier to slip into the habit of comparison. You can't compare your life to the highlight reel of someone else's life that they post on social media. Every person on this earth struggles, but not everyone is going to share that. We seem to get into comparison mode when we're not feeling great about ourselves. Be honest…how many times have you had a bad day and got on some social platform and scrolled, only to end up feeling worse?

Here's a bit of homework: Go through your social media accounts and unfollow any account that makes you feel bad about yourself. Even if you think you're following for "inspiration," if you feel bad about yourself after looking at their content, unfollow them now. You have the right to curate your social feeds to become spaces that *contribute* to your mental health, rather than detract from it. Worried about unfollowing or blocking people? Mute them for a while. How does your world change after a week or two of not seeing their content? If you feel better, you know what to do.

4. Take a break.

Sometimes a change of scenery or a change of pace is good for your mental wellbeing. It could be a five-minute pause from cleaning your kitchen, a half-hour lunch break at work, or a weekend exploring somewhere new. It could be getting out in your garden, jumping on the treadmill, or lying on the floor for a few minutes and taking some deep breaths before you hop on your next Zoom call. Taking a break may mean being active, or it may mean not doing much at all. You know what you need. If you're feeling lethargic, try moving around for a while. If after ten to fifteen minutes you feel more tired, you could probably use some sleep. Listen to your body. Give it what it's asking for. The more you listen to what your body needs, the more feelings of safety you create for yourself, and the more your nervous system will calm down.

5. Learn how to manage your time and focus your energy.

Research conducted at Stanford University[47] has shown that multitasking kills your performance and can damage your brain. As much as we might like to pride ourselves on being taskmasters, in reality, our brain can only focus on one task at a time. When we try to do two things at once, we lack the capacity to perform either task well.

What if you feel you have a special gift for multitasking? Stanford researchers compared groups of people based on their tendency to multitask and their belief that it helps their performance. They found that heavy multitaskers—those who multitask a lot and feel that it boosts their performance—were actually *less productive* than those who like to do a single thing at a time.

Multitasking can also affect your gray matter. Researchers at the University of Sussex[48] compared the time people spend on multiple devices (such as texting while watching TV) to MRI scans of their brains. They found high multitaskers had less brain density in the anterior cingulate cortex, a region responsible for empathy and cognitive and emotional control. While more research is needed to determine if multitasking damages the brain (versus whether it is existing brain damage that predisposes people to multitask), it's clear that multitasking has negative effects. This amount of decreased productivity can cause more stress, which will affect your mental and physical health. So how do you get around this?

- **Time blocking.**

  Focus on one task at a time. Set a timer for yourself to get it done. I use this in my work life and personal life and it's made a *massive* difference in my productivity and peace of mind. I choose one task and set a timer on my phone for thirty minutes, then get to work on *that one thing only.* I do not work on anything else during that time,

---

[47] Adam Gorlick, "Media Multitaskers Pay Mental Price, Stanford Study Shows," Stanford News, Aug. 24, 2009, https://news.stanford.edu/news/2009/august24/multitask-research-study-082409.html.
[48] "Brain Scans Reveal 'Gray Matter' Differences in Media Multitaskers," EurekAlert!, Sept. 24, 2014, https://www.eurekalert.org/news-releases/467495.

and will not check text messages or emails or take phone calls. Nine times out of ten, I complete the task before my timer runs out. Then I choose the next task and do the same thing. I can get more done in less time, and have more time for play! Try this out and see how it works for you. Remember, add in time for something just for your own enjoyment. Even thirty minutes of me-time can make a vast difference.

• Do something you're good at.

What do you really love doing? Which activities can you lose yourself in? Doing an activity you're good at and accomplishing something can boost your self-esteem. Concentrating on a hobby you enjoy can free your mind and reduce stress. It's a beautiful thing to have an activity where you're not someone's parent, supervisor, caretaker, or employee...something where you can just be yourself. Not sure where to start? Think about what you used to enjoy before you got caught up in the busyness of life. What activities used to bring you joy and light you up? Start there. Or explore something new, outside your comfort zone, and be present in the experience of it.

• Be gentle with yourself.

This one is *hard* for people-pleasers, because we're perfectionists. But here's some real talk: *perfection does not exist*. Period. One of the hardest, best things you can learn is how to show yourself compassion and *give yourself a break*. Give yourself permission to be messy and imperfect, and treat yourself with kindness. When you can be your own best friend and cheerleader, everything changes. In the next section, we'll go over a few ways you can reprogram your mind to be gentler with yourself.

• Recognize your limits.

When your phone gets low on battery power, what do you do? You charge it, right? Chances are you're recharging your phone every day. Well, believe it or not, we need that same time to recharge each day so we can continue our work in the world. However, so many of us are running on empty, trying to squeeze a day's worth of energy out of our last little bit of battery life. We allow ourselves to recharge just enough to get by, but never refill our whole tank. Then we give, give, give from our own depleted energy stores until there's nothing left. This is an unhealthy cycle that can lead to burnout—and much worse.

People have ended up in the hospital from burning themselves out, suffering from exhaustion or from more debilitating diseases because they ignored their symptoms in order to keep going. There's only so much you can do in a day, and only so much energy you can spend before you need to recharge. It's important that you allow yourself time to recharge, so you can give to others from your overflow instead of from your vital life force. Part of rebuilding your life is learning where your limits are. How many hours can you work until you need a break? How long can you stay in a conversation until you get tired? How can you share tasks so you are not doing everything yourself? Where are your physical, mental, and emotional limits? Enforce your boundaries, delegate certain tasks, ask for help, and structure your time in a way that is conducive to your success in all aspects of life—and take time to recharge.

6. Manage your worries.

One practice I've found helpful is to write my list of important things to accomplish the next day before I go to bed so they're not swirling around in my head all night. If you're thinking of things for multiple days, write them down stream-of-consciousness style on a comprehensive list (the "brain dump"), or write them all down on your calendar. Whatever you can do to clear your head before bedtime will help you have a restful sleep.

*

SPIRIT

Humankind has not woven the web of life. We are but one thread within it. Whatever we do to the web, we do to ourselves. All things are bound together. All things connect.

—Chief Seattle, Suquamish and Duwamish Chief

Spirituality means something different to every individual, and so it should. Your spiritual life is a personal experience. No matter whom or what you believe in, it's important to recognize and have faith in a power greater than yourself. Spirituality of all kinds nurtures your soul and opens the door to love, safety, and wonder. Having a spiritual foundation can help you weather the storms of life, knowing you are guided by something bigger than your human experience.

When you explore the terrain of your personal spirituality, a Higher Power will reach out to meet your efforts. There's a beautiful restoration that happens when you reclaim your power from other people and put your faith in the force that animates our universe. You see the world and yourself differently, and can rest easy knowing that in the eyes of the Higher Power, you are enough. You don't have to prove your worth to the universe. You don't have to bend. You can just be. Spirituality can help us generate purpose, peace, and forgiveness in our lives.

Purpose

A person who lives in a state of unity with the Source of all life doesn't look any different from ordinary folks.
These people don't wear a halo or dress in special garments that announce their godlike qualities.
But when you notice that they go through life as the lucky ones who seem to get all the breaks, and when you begin to talk to them, you realize how distinctive they are compared to people living at ordinary levels of awareness.[49]

—Wayne Dyer, *The Power of Intention*

---

[49] Wayne Dyer, *The Power of Intention* (Hay House Inc., Dec. 15, 2005).

What I realized along this journey is that when we are entrenched in people-pleasing , we give away our power. We make others our Source— of love, of praise, of affirmation, and of safety. When we do this, we allow others to guide the ship of our lives, rather than setting the course ourselves.

Picture this—you're at the helm of a large ship, holding the wheel steady. Someone grabs the wheel, and pulls it to the left. Another person pulls it to the right...a third person jams the throttle full ahead, and a fourth tries to put the boat into reverse. All the while, you're trying to redirect the ship back on the original course you'd set. This is what it's like in your life when you are people-pleasing and have no boundaries. You get pulled in a million different directions and waste your time and energy fighting to get back on track, when you could simply avoid the whole mess to begin with.

The biggest lesson I've learned on this journey is the power of living with intention. Not only that, I've learned to keep myself on course, and to protect my path and my peace. So many things in life have the potential to take you off track and distract you, it's imperative to learn two things—first, the laws of the universe we live in, and second, how to have them work in your favor.

The Twelve Laws of the Universe

Understanding the laws of the universe shows us how to master life on many levels and gives us a roadmap of how to live our best and most purposeful lives. The twelve laws of the universe are thought to be intrinsic, unchanging laws of our universe that ancient cultures have always known.

1. Law of Divine Oneness

This law states that we are all connected through creation – that everything we do in life creates a ripple effect that impacts the collective - not just ourselves. It means that everything we do, big or small, matters and makes a difference.

How to apply it:

The application of this particular law can get a bit cerebral, but to break it down, we can apply this law by being compassionate to others. Ask yourself how you could try to understand people you don't see eye to eye with, or "what would Love do?" Just be careful to maintain balance and your boundaries while exploring these questions.

2. Law of Vibration

Everything in this universe has a certain frequency and vibration to it. Nothing ever stands still... the entire universe is in a constant state of motion, with everything being constantly drawn towards and pushed away from others. Items of a similar frequency are drawn together.

How to apply it:

If you want to manifest (bring into your life) things and experiences that you desire, do things that will make your personal frequency match that of what you desire by feeling gratitude and/or "acting as if" you already have them in your life.

3. Law of Correspondence

This law states that patterns repeat throughout the universe, and that on a personal level, our reality is a mirror of what is happening inside of us at that moment. "As above, so below. As within, so without."

How to apply it:

Remember that life is happening *for you,* not *to you.* If you encounter a troubling situation in your life, ask yourself what this situation is here to show you about yourself.

4. Law of Attraction

This law is basically the law of vibration in action. It says that like attracts like, and that what you focus on you get more of... whether it's positive or negative.

How to apply it:

At any point in time, you can change your mindset and make different decisions, which will ultimately change your vibration and start attracting people and things that are on a similar positive frequency.

5. Law of Inspired Action

Building on the law of attraction, the law of inspired action is about taking real, actionable steps to bring what we want into our lives. It's about following that gentle, intuitive nudge to act, not necessarily making a plan of action.

How to apply it:

Slow down and get quiet, creating space for yourself to hear your internal guidance. Refer back to the meditation and mindfulness practices in Chapter 5 to quiet your mind, and open yourself to all possibilities. You'll be surprised at the ideas you get when you're in the flow.

6. Law of Perpetual Transmutation of Energy

This law states that even the smallest action can have a profound effect. Every action is preceded by a thought, and thoughts have the power to manifest in our physical reality when they are repeated for a long enough period of time.

How to apply it:

To put yourself on a positive track, do small things each day that uplift you. Small shifts can add up to major results over time. A great place to start is with a gratitude practice – simply jotting down things you're grateful for in a notebook every day. You'd be amazed at how this simple practice can change the course of your life if you stick with it.

7. Law of Cause and Effect

Also known as the law of karma, the law of cause and effect states that any action causes a reaction. We often can't see the effects right away, but they will come back around.

How to apply it:

Be aware of how your actions and decisions are affecting not just yourself, but everyone around you. Also be aware of the energetic underpinning of your actions. For example, if you are doing something "good," but feel resentful while doing it, that *resentful* energy is what is going to come back to you. It's all about your intention and the *true* energy behind your actions that matters.

8. Law of Compensation

The law of compensation states that you reap what you sow. Compensation in this sense isn't limited to employment or financial compensation. It's about receiving compensation for *all* your contributions to the world around you, including the love, joy, and kindness you spread. It's all rewarded in unique ways.

How to apply it:

Move through your day being conscious of the energy you're putting out into the world. *Choose* to help and serve others from a place of overflow, and spread love and kindness everywhere you go. Something as simple as smiling at someone or holding a door open can go a long way.

9. Law of Relativity

This law suggests that we are inclined to compare and label things in our world, but in reality, everything is neutral. The meaning we give things depends on our perspective and perception.

How to apply it:

Applying this law can help us to understand the tougher parts of life with greater compassion. For example, rather than fretting about what isn't working in our lives, we can change our focus to being grateful for what is working and what we already have.

10. Law of Polarity

The law of polarity states that everything in the universe has a polar opposite and that there are two sides to each coin… light and dark, warm and cold, good and evil.

How to apply it:

Experiencing these polarities is part of the human journey. You can work with the mantra *contrast brings clarity* to remind yourself of this law. The polarities of our life experiences help us to learn from our mistakes and support us in identifying what we don't want, so we can gain clarity about what we *do* want.

11. Law of Rhythm

This law states that everything is forever changing, and that all things come in cycles. We see this in nature with the changing of seasons and the body's aging process.

How to apply it:

We can apply this law to the stages of our life. Today's season may be good, but nothing lasts forever, so enjoy the good times while they're here without trying to extend them beyond what is natural. On the other hand, if you're experiencing a negative cycle, it may be the very thing preparing you for a prosperous change in cycles next month.

12. Law of Gender

The law of gender has very little to do with biological sex. Rather, it states that there are two major forms of energy that make up this universe, and us as humans. We can refer to these energies as masculine and feminine, as yin and yang, or as anima and animus.

How to apply it:

We all contain a certain amount of each of these energies, and must find a way to achieve a balance between both in order to live authentically and happily. Think about the roles each of these energies plays in your life, and whether you have an excess or a deficit of either. Then you can find ways to balance these two energies in yourself.

*

What I realized as I did this work was that I was actually afraid of the power that lived inside of me. I was afraid of how my full ownership and wielding of my personal power would be perceived. I was worried about being the "too much" chick. I was worried that if I showed my entire self to the world, I would be shunned, abandoned, and end up alone.

Isn't that the quintessential fear we as a human family share? The fear of being alone? It's a primal fear that lives in our DNA. It has lived inside us for generations upon generations. That fear makes us look to the outside world for validation, love, companionship, sustenance, and proof

161

that we exist and matter. Really, we can give all of that to ourselves and learn to receive what we need from the Higher Power. When you reclaim power over your existence from the external world and turn it over to the Higher Power, something magical happens. You tap into a limitless supply of love, energy, wellness, and sustenance of every kind. When you prioritize your inner world, you build a strong foundation upon which you can build great, immovable towers.

Here's a visualization to illustrate this point:

Imagine you are looking at yourself in the mirror and you see cords coming off of you and going out into the world in a bunch of directions. Some cords go to your work and the people there, others to your family and friends, others to your pets, your social media accounts, your phone, your computer, etc. These are the cords you send out into the world, and each one carries some of your energy... your life force. When you are looking to the external world for validation, you are sending out cords and siphoning your own energy out in all these different directions. This can leave you feeling drained, burnt out. However, if you disconnect all these cords from the people and situations outside of yourself and plug them back into the Higher Power, you allow yourself to be *refilled and replenished.* You open up to receive true unconditional love, unlimited energy and supply, and peace.

I've created a special meditation track that leads you through this practice to recall all of your energy back into your own body. You can find it at www.doitforyoubook.com/resources.[50]

Peace

I'll never forget the moment I felt complete, profound inner peace after decades of running. My life had blown up around me. The chaos and pain felt insurmountable. I did not know what I was doing. I cried out to the universe "Show me what's real. Guide me." I was enveloped in a wave lov-

---

[50] Vanessa Ooms, "Call Your Energy Back," Do It For You, Oct. 29, 2022, https://www.doitforyoubook.com/resources/call-your-energy-back.

ing, comforting energy. I realized I didn't need these relationships. I had become nothing and was okay with it. I could lean into this Higher Power that had enveloped me and receive everything I needed. I didn't have to seek outside of myself for anything—this powerful force lived within me. It *was* me. And *that* became all I needed.

Whether we're shopping, posting to social media, eating, or snuggling, we're all seeking inner peace. We hope that a new purse will ease our anxiety, or that we can be validated through enough likes on our posts, or that we can be comforted by food. In these pursuits we're seeking peace...the peace that comes through loving ourselves and believing we live in a benevolent universe.

Choose What You Trust.

One revelation that brought me peace was that I get to choose what I trust. When I trusted that the people around me would treat me with respect, hold my heart, or have my best interests in mind, and then I found out that wasn't the case, I suffered. I took it personally, thinking I didn't matter or that the people were malicious. While sometimes people *are* malicious, I realized I had high expectations of others and of myself. None of us could live up to them. We're all doing the best we can with what we know. We're all seeking love and to end our suffering. The way others choose to relieve their suffering sometimes is to transfer that suffering onto others.

I trusted in the Higher Power of our universe (rather than in people), and it brought me profound peace. After I made that commitment, astonishing things manifested in my life. The most amazing thing was a deep sense of safety and security. I knew I would always be looked after, even if things and people needed to fall out of my life. I stopped looking to other people to validate me and instead looked to the Higher Power to reflect my worth back to me. As I built my spiritual foundation of trust in the universe, things shifted in my external reality. My relationships with other human beings deepened. I became more vulnerable, healthier, and my *need* to have others see and validate me dissolved. I started making more life-affirming choices in business and in my finances because I stopped waiting around for someone to fix these things for me. Walking with the Higher Power straightened my spine, so to speak, and made me respect myself. The more I respected myself, the more others respected me—and the less I cared whether others respected me. I stopped caring so much about what other people thought of me or my life because I was being led by my higher guidance—and it felt fantastic!

Choosing what you trust in this life brings a sense of peace and empowerment that is hard to describe. Explore this for yourself and see what resonates with you.

Forgive.

Forgiveness is one of the most powerful spiritual healing tools I've ever come across, and it's not what you think. Forgiveness is not letting people off the hook for treating you poorly, but deciding that you will no longer allow their actions to have a hold on your mind, emotions, or life. It's setting yourself free. When we feel that someone has wronged us, we can hold on to resentment. When we continue to speak about *the things that happened to us* and our feelings about it, we hold ourselves in spiritual bondage. We keep this situation and the related negative emotions active in our minds and spirits and transfer this into the minds and spirits of those with whom we share it. Because we are focused on the past, we end up blocking ourselves off from resolution and from positive opportunities that come our way in life. Our resentments suck the life out of our present moment and make us miss the beauty and magic available to us *right now.*

In order to move forward and release yourself from that bondage, you've got to forgive. Let's be clear—forgiveness doesn't mean you condone the other person's behavior. You do not have to be okay with how you were mistreated. When you forgive, you are untangling yourself from the other person. You're releasing yourself from the memories, from the emotional triggers of those memories, and from the expectation that the other person is going to change.

Sometimes forgiveness is accepting the fact that you might not get an apology or find a resolution with the other person. It's accepting that the other person might never acknowledge that they mistreated you, and might never see it. It's releasing yourself from the *hope* that they might change. The good news is that you don't have to have a conversation with that person to find a resolution. You can go into your meditation, into your imagination, and have the conversation with them you want to have. Envision yourself facing the other person and saying all the things you need to say, and see them in your mind saying all the things you need to hear from them. Allow yourself to feel the relief and the resolution in your body, and give yourself closure. It might sound wacky, but this practice is powerful.

After you forgive others, you can forgive yourself. In the previous Chapter, we talked about having compassion for ourselves and re-parenting ourselves. Forgiving yourself for past mistakes is paramount to releasing feelings of shame and regret. Recognize that you were doing the best you could with what you knew at the time. Notice where you had porous boundaries (or no boundaries), and learn from those experiences. Do better for yourself next time. But see yourself with compassion and love, because we all make mistakes. There's not one person on this beautiful planet of ours who hasn't screwed up or hurt someone else. It's part of being human. Human beings are fallible and imperfect. Forgiving yourself frees you from the trap of perfectionism and gives you the space to learn, grow, and evolve.

Approach Life with a Beginner's Mind

The mind of the beginner is empty, free of the habits of the expert,
ready to accept, to doubt, and open to all the possibilities.
It is the kind of mind which can see things as they are,
which step by step and, in a flash, can realize the original nature
of everything.[51]

—Shunryu Suzuki, Zen Mind, Beginner's Mind

Remember what it was like to learn something new as a kid? It's sometimes confusing, and you look at everything with curiosity and wonder. This is the premise of the Zen mind, or beginner's mind—to look at every life experience with a sense of wonder, as if you're seeing it and experiencing it for the first time. It's the ultimate practice of presence and can

---

[51] Shunryu Suzuki, *Zen Mind, Beginner's Mind: Informal Talks on Zen Meditation and Practice* (Colorado: Shambala Publications, Inc., 1970).

be pivotal in cultivating a sense of peace. In our modern world, it can be easy to get distracted by the barrage of information coming at us. We move through our world on autopilot, taking our blessings for granted and forgetting to savor the beautiful moments we get each day. When we practice beginner's mind, time slows down. We tap into a greater sense of ease, abundance, and wonder as we witness the exquisite miracle that is Life on Earth.

Practicing a beginner's mind can reduce anxiety, improve our relationships, and enhance most other life experiences, because we are dropping our preconceived judgments and expectations and approaching each situation and person with an open, curious mind. For instance, if you have an upcoming event or big meeting you are anxious about, instead of worrying about what might happen, let go of your preconceived ideas. Embrace not knowing. Be present in the moment, curious about who you're meeting, and what is about to happen. Remain open to all possibilities.

Embracing life with this attitude makes every part of life sacred. Rather than judging situations and people as "good" or "bad," you see everything and everyone as multi-dimensional and having many aspects.

Tap Into the Power of Intention

As you navigate your new reality, I encourage you to approach all things with a beginner's mind and to integrate your intention into every action. What does this mean? It means to approach everything you do with a strong purpose or aim, accompanied by a determination to produce a desired result. But it's more than a mental game. Driven people are *inspired* or *in-spirited*. They are filled with Spirit. They are tapped into forces that animate our universe and are operating on a high frequency. The beginner's mind and a meditation practice allow us to remove all distractions and get into the present moment, where Spirit lives. When we are tapped in like this, we allow ourselves to be *filled with the Spirit*. When we are inspired in such a way, anything is possible.

Whether they are conscious or unconscious, our intentions direct the course of our lives. When recovering from people-pleasing, we are learning to train ourselves away from unconscious intentions to get the needs of our Shadow met and toward guiding our intentions and relating in a healthy manner with ourselves and others. We can take that a step further and *intend* to bring light, peace, and openness into every situation we encounter. We can *intend* to hold space for others, to have strong boundaries, and to create a different life for ourselves.

Your focused intentions hold great power and great creative potential. In order to tap into the full potential of focused intention, you must live in integrity. Aligning your actions with your thoughts and words removes any static from your energy and creates an open channel for you to be *inspired*. When you create and interact from that space, amazing transformation can happen for you personally and for all of your relations. Say what you mean, do what you say you're going to do (keeping your promises to yourself as well), honor your intuition, trust your instincts, and you will go far.

A great place to start is to intend for synchronicity in every area of your life. You can write down your mantra and put it somewhere you will see it multiple times a day, reminding yourself that "I intend to create synchronicity in all areas of my life." Check in with yourself often. Are the actions you take in line with your intention? If they aren't, adjust. Have compassion for yourself as you navigate this new awareness and new reality.

Your whole life is a practice of refinement. Keep going.

And just like that, one day I gave up on all of my excuses
and began to light the fuses.
—Jonathon Muncy Storm (JmStorm)

If you enjoyed this book, please take a moment to review it on Amazon or GoodReads. Every review is appreciated.

SUPPLEMENTAL MATERIAL

As mentioned at the beginning of this book, I've compiled some supplemental material to guide you along the healing journey laid out in this book. They include:

- Guided meditation videos

- Do It for You Book Club — an online gathering where we come together to go through the content of this book and share our experiences along the way.

- A downloadable list of affirmations you can print out and tape to your mirror

- Printable journaling prompts for self-discovery on many different topics

You can find these resources at www.doitforyoubook.com/resources. Use the password DIFY to access your materials.

Wishing you a beautiful, deep and transformative journey.

Much love,
V

ACKNOWLEDGEMENTS

I respectfully acknowledge that I live, work and play on the Unceded Traditional Territory of the K'ómoks First Nation. I am grateful to be here, interacting with the land and ancestors with great honor and reverence.

There are so many people who came out of the woodwork to support me on this journey, and others who came through my life to trigger me and challenge me to embody these teachings even deeper as I wrote. I thank you all.

Big thanks to my family, soul fam and amazing friends for your unconditional support and encouragement, no matter what kind of crazy ideas I pitch to you. You're always my safe place, and I love you all so much!

Gratitude to the Invisible Grace who worked through my YouTube community to support me in the creation of this book. This project wouldn't have come to fruition without you.

Huge thanks to Michael Ireland for your editing prowess and thorough guidance. Thank you for helping me structure this book into a professional project that I can be proud of.

And deep appreciation for all of the masters, teachers, healers, medicine people and way-showers who have walked this path before me. Thank you for leaving your imprints on the planet and in our consciousness.

GLOSSARY OF TERMS

Abuse - treating someone with cruelty or violence regularly and repeatedly. This includes physical abuse, mental abuse, emotional abuse and spiritual abuse.

Alchemy - transforming one thing into something else. *Used in this book:* emotional alchemy, or transforming the energy of one emotion into the energy of another.

Anxiety - feeling worried, nervous, uneasy or exceedingly apprehensive

Attachment - the feeling of a bond or connection between two people or between a person and their feelings or memories.

Autopilot Mind - acting or reacting without thinking about what you're doing, usually because you've done it many times before.

Chanting - saying or singing words or phrases in a singsong tone. Often practiced with sacred texts or phrases, but can also be practiced with affirmations.

Codependent - an imbalanced relating style where one person is excessively reliant on the other, and the other enables their self-destructive or abusive behavior.

Cognitive Behavioral Therapy (CBT) - a talking therapy that can help you manage your problems by changing the way you think and behave.

Consciousness - the state of being awake and aware of your surroundings. Also, the awareness the mind has of itself and of the world.

Cortisol - the primary stress hormone created by the adrenal gland. While it can be helpful in fight-or-flight situations, high levels of cortisol in the body due to prolonged stress can cause a lot of different health issues.

Counter-dependent - an imbalanced relating style where the person resists asking for help and seeks to be completely self-reliant. Counter-dependents lack trust in others and fear the consequences of doing so.

Creator - a name used for God. *See God for definition.*

Depression - consistent feelings of sadness and apathy that interfere with your daily life. Can range from mild to sever symptoms and accompany various other symptoms, from difficulty making decisions to fatigue to suicidal thoughts.

Dis-ease - an alternative to the word *disease* that means a "lack of ease" in the body. It alludes to the natural state of ease, or homeostasis, that our body tends toward.

Dopamine - a chemical in the body that is responsible for allowing you to feel pleasure, satisfaction and motivation.

Ego - the "I" or "self" of any person. Your conscious mind and consciousness of your own identity. The idea or opinion that you have of yourself. Everyone has an ego, whether big or small. Ego can become a problem when it becomes overpowering.

Emotion - instinctive or intuitive feelings. Also, *energy in motion*. Emotions float through us on a daily basis. They can become toxic if we hold them in and make stories about them, rather than letting them flow through our body like they are intended to do.

Emotional Alchemy - transforming the energy of one emotion into the energy of another.

Emotional Body - the bridge between the mental and physical bodies. Where our experience of the world is synthesized and interpreted. It represents our feelings and relationship to all things. *If you're interested in exploring this more, research the 5 Koshas in the yogic tradition.*

Emotional signature - the emotional imprint of a memory or experience. Also, the predictable way that we react to certain situations or triggers. Our emotional signature can change over time when we do *the work* on ourselves.

Empath - someone who is highly attuned to the feelings and emotions of those around them. Often empaths will feel the emotions of others in their own body as if they are their own emotions. It can be difficult for the empath to discern where they end and the other person/people begin.

Energetic body - your body has an electromagnetic field around it, also called a "biofield," that is composed of 5 energy bodies (koshas) and 7 main energy centers (chakras). Because the frequencies of the biofield cannot be seen with the naked eye, the energetic body is often also called the subtle energy body. *If you're interested in exploring this more, research the 5 Koshas in the yogic tradition.*

Energetic signature - the distinctive way that a person's energy is felt and expressed. Sometimes a person's energetic signature is so strong that it can shift the energy of an entire room.

Energy - life force, prana, soul energy...they all mean the same thing. Every single part of this universe, including you, are made up of energy. It's what holds our atoms together, what creates great winds, and also great transformation.

Energy in motion - another word for emotion or e-motion.

Energy vampire - a person who, sometimes intentionally, drains your emotional energy. They feed on your willingness to listen to them and care for them, leaving you exhausted and overwhelmed.

Eye Movement Desensitization Reprocessing (EMDR) - therapy developed in the late 1980's to treat PTSD. EMDR changes the way that traumatic memories are stored in the brain, which in turn can reduce PTSD symptoms.

False self - the facade that is created to appease the people around us. It's a mask made out of what we *think* others will like or accept. Often it's very different from our true self.

Gaslighting - a manipulation tactic meant to make a person question their own sanity. For example, and abusive person telling their partner that they are irrational until they start think it must be true.

God - the invisible, omnipresent, omniscient force that animates every part of this universe. So massive and all encompassing that it surpasses all labels.

Grounded / Staying Grounded - remaining mentally and emotionally stable, sensible, realistic and unpretentious.

Healing - *in this book*: overcoming limiting beliefs, abuse, traumatic memories and negative self talk and making your way toward your best life.

Healing Eruptions - spontaneous waves of energy and emotion that can happen during your healing process. Sometimes they happen because of an obvious event that is happening in our lives currently, but other times a healing eruption can seem to come out of nowhere, because we've made a subconscious and internal breakthrough, and this unlocks a mass of stored energy that needs to move through the body to be processed and released.

Heart rate variability - when the amount of time between heartbeats fluctuates slightly.

Higher Power - another name for God. *See God for definition.*

Hold space / holding space - being physically, mentally and emotionally present for someone. Putting your complete focus on someone to support them in as they feel their feelings and talk things out.

Inner light - your true soul essence. Who you really are. *See also True Self.*

Intimacy - when you can show all of yourself to someone—the good, the bad, and the ugly—and be loved for it all.

Love-bombing - a manipulation tactic in which a person will lavish you with attention, affection, compliments and gifts to overwhelm you. This is done to sweep you up in positive emotions so that you will ignore red flags and become oblivious to their underlying abusive behavior.

Manifestation - to bring something into your reality by making yourself a vibrational match to it. This is a conscious manifestation, but we also manifest unconsciously… attracting things and situations that are a vibrational match to our limiting beliefs and past patterns.

Meditation - remaining in a silent and calm state for a period of time so that you are more able to deal with the problems of daily life.

Mindfulness - focusing your awareness on the present moment, while calmly and consciously acknowledging and accepting your feelings, thoughts and bodily sensations.

Move it through your body - a term used to describe moving energy and emotions (energy in motion) through your body and out of your system. More often than not, this will include actually moving your physical body, whether it's walking, dancing, shaking, crying, etc.

Narcissist - someone who is so self-involved that they ignore the needs of those around them. Others often describe people with Narcissistic Personality Disorder as cocky, manipulative, selfish, patronizing and demanding. Narcissists are extremely resistant to changing their behavior, even when it's causing problems. They tend to blame others instead.

Non-attachment - a heightened perspective in which a person overcomes their emotional attachment to or desire for things, people or worldly concerns.

Observer Mind - the practice of becoming aware of your thoughts.

Panic Attack - sudden episode of intense fear that triggers sever physical reactions when there is no real danger or apparent cause.

Parasympathetic Nervous System - network of nerves that relaxes your body after periods of stress or danger.

People Pleaser - someone who has an emotional need to please others, often at the expense of their own needs and desires.

Physical Body - the organic, physical structure of your body.

Prayer - a spiritual communion with God in which you speak freely, express thanks, ask for help, etc. A very personal experience and relationship.

Safe space - a space where a person feels comfortable to express themselves freely and be received with unconditional love and acceptance.

Shadow / Shadow Self - the unknown dark side of the personality that is comprised of all the aspects that one deems undesirable and unloveable.

Shadow Work - working with your subconscious mind to uncover the parts of yourself that you repress and hide from yourself.

Soul - the spiritual or immaterial part of a person or animal that is regarded as immortal.

Source - another word for God. *See God for definition.*

Spirit - another word for God or the Holy Spirit. *See God for definition.*

Spiritual Body - also known as the Astral Body in yogic tradition, it is the electromagnetic field, aura or energetic body that surrounds and encompasses a being's physical body.

Subconscious Mind - the data bank for everything that is beneath the focus of your conscious mind. Includes your beliefs, previous experiences, memories, and learned skills that have become automatic.

Surrender - release the need to control the outcomes of your life and trust that everything is working out the way it should.

Sympathetic Nervous System - network of nerves that activates the body in response to dangerous or stressful situations.

Systemic Constellations Therapy - a way of working with issues within human systems that acknowledges the existence of a collective energy field that connects groups of people.

Trigger / Emotional Trigger - anything that sparks an intense emotional reaction such as memories, experiences or events.

Toxic - poisonous; very harmful or unpleasant in a pervasive or insidious way.

True Self - the one who lives behind the masks, the expectations, the doing, and the order. *See also Inner Light.*

Unconscious Mind - another name for Subconscious Mind. *See Subconscious Mind for definition.*

Vagal Tone - a measurement of activity of the vagus nerve and of cardiovascular function that shows adaptive responses to environmental challenges.

Vagus Nerve - also known as the vagal nerves, this is the main network of nerves of the parasympathetic nervous system.

Work or "the work" - process of remaining alert to and questioning stressful thoughts. It's a simple, powerful and effective meditation practice.

BIBLIOGRAPHY

American Psychiatric Association. *Diagnostic and Statistical Manual of Mental Disorders: DSM-5*. 5th ed 2013.

Angelou, Maya. Interview by Bill Moyers, Moyers & Company, 1973.

Beckwith, Michael Bernard. *Spiritual Liberation: Fulfilling Your Soul's Potential*. Atria Books/Beyond Words, Nov. 8, 2008.

Bloch, Jena and Ed. "Mind Matters - Parental Mirroring Provides Child Sense of Self-Worth." Lawrence Journal-World, 2011. https://www2.ljworld.com/news/2011/dec/05/mind-matters-parental-mirroring-provides-child-sen/.

Bolte Taylor, Jill. *My Stroke of Insight: A Brain Scientist's Personal Journey*. New York: Penguin Group, 2009.

Borenstein, Jeffrey, M.D.. "Self-Love and What It Means." Brain & Behavior, February 12, 2020. https://www.bbrfoundation.org/blog/self-love-and-what-it-means.

"Brain Scans Reveal 'Gray Matter' Differences in Media Multitaskers." EurekAlert!, Sept. 24, 2014. https://www.eurekalert.org/news-releases/467495.

Brown, Brené. *Braving the Wilderness: The Quest for True Belonging and the Courage to Stand Alone*. New York: Random House, 2019.

Cambridge Dictionary. "Opinion." accessed Jun 13, 2022. https://dictionary.cambridge.org/dictionary/english/opinion.

Chapman, Benjamin P., Kevin Fiscella, Ichiro Kawachi, Paul Duberstein, and Peter Muennig. "Emotion Suppression and Mortality Risk Over a 12-Year Follow-Up," Journal of Psychosomatic Research, Volume 75, Issue 4 (2013): 381-385, ISSN 0022-3999. https://doi.org/10.1016/j.jpsychores.2013.07.014.

Clancy, Jennifer A., Susan A Deuchars, Jim Deuchars. "The Wonders of the Wanderer." National Library of Medicine, 2013. https://pubmed.ncbi.nlm.nih.gov/22848084/.

Cuncic, Arlin. "What is Imposter Syndrome?." Very Well Mind, updated on October 22, 2022. https://www.verywellmind.com/imposter-syndrome-and-social-anxiety-disorder-4156469.

Didion, Joan. "Quotable Quote." Good Reads, Accessed July 9, 2022. https://www.goodreads.com/quotes/7330826-i-have-already-lost-touch-with-a-couple-of-people.

Dispenza, Joe. *Breaking the Habit of Being Yourself: How to Lose Your Mind and Create a New One*. Hay House Inc., 2013.

Dispenza, Joe. "The Role of Brainwaves in Meditation: Part I." Unlimited Joe Dispenza, Dec. 12, 2020. https://drjoedispenza.com/blogs/dr-joes-blog/the-role-of-brainwaves-in-meditation-part-i.

"Doctor Explains How to Relieve Anxiety Instantly Using Your Vagus Nerve." Power of Positivity, 2017. https://www.powerofpositivity.com/relieve-anxiety-vagus-nerve/.

Dyer, Wayne. *The Power of Intention*. Hay House Inc., Dec. 15, 2005.

"Emily McDowell Quotes." GoodReads. https://www.goodreads.com/quotes/9586181-finding-yourself-is-not-really-how-it-works-you-aren-t.

"Family Constellation." Hellinger Schule. https://www.hellinger.com/en/family-constellation/.

"Family Constellations." Wikipedia. https://en.wikipedia.org/wiki/Family_Constellations.

Gorlick, Adam. "Media Multitaskers Pay Mental Price, Stanford Study Shows." Stanford News, Aug. 24, 2009. https://news.stanford.edu/news/2009/august24/multitask-research-study-082409.html.

Harrison, Tracy. "Surprising Interconnectedness: Functional Medicine Insights on Complex Issues." The School of Applied Functional Medicine, July 13 2018. https://schoolafm.com/ws_clinical_know/functional-medicine-insights-on-complex-issues/.

Hay, Louise. Heal Your Body: *The Mental Causes for Physical illness and the Metaphysical Way to Overcome Them*. Hay House Inc., Jan. 1, 1984.

Hay, Louise. *Mirror Work: 21 Days to Heal Your Life*. Hay House Inc., March 22, 2016.

Hay, Louise. *You Can Heal Your Life*. Hay House Inc., 1984.

Hof, Wim. "Vagus Nerve Stimulation." Wim Hof Method. https://www.wimhofmethod.com/vagus-nerve-stimulation.

Jestine. "Stream of Consciousness: A Different Take on Journaling." Rediscover Analog, November 14, 2019. http://rediscoveranalog.com/stream-of-consciousness-a-different-take-on-journaling/.

Jonas, Wayne. M.D.. "Use Exercise to Increase Your Body's Ability to Heal." Psychology Today, Dec. 30, 2019. https://www.psychologytoday.com/ca/blog/how-healing-works/201912/use-exercise-increase-your-body-s-ability-heal.

Jung, Carl. *Aion: Researches Into the Phenomenology of the Self.* Routledge & Kagan Paul Ltd, 1959.

LaChance, Laura R and Drew Ramsey. "Antidepressant Foods: An Evidence-Based Nutrient Profiling System For Depression." National Library of Medicine, Sept. 20, 2018. https://www.ncbi.nlm.nih.gov/pmc/articles/PMC6147775.

Manson, Mark. *The Subtle Art of Not Giving a F*ck: A Counterintuitive Approach to Living a Good Life.* New York: HarperCollins Publishers, 2016.

Miguel Ruiz, Don. *The Four Agreements: A Practical Guide to Personal Freedom.* Amber-Allen Publishing, 1997.

Newton, Melanie. "How to Harness the Five Types of Assertion to Get Your Voice Heard." Business Business Business, accessed on Sept. 12, 2022. https://www.business-businessbusiness.com.au/harness-five-types-assertion-get-voice-heard/.

Northrup, Christiane. *Dodging Energy Vampires: An Empath's Guide to Evading Relationships That Drain You and Restoring Your Health and Power.* New York: Hay House, Inc., 2018.

Norwood, Robin. *Women Who Love Too Much: When You Keep Wishing and Hoping He'll Change.* New York: Pocket Books, A Division of Simon & Schuster, Inc., 1985.

Oelze, Patricia. "What is Cognitive Behavioural Therapy?." Better Help, August 26, 2022. https://www.betterhelp.com/advice/therapy/what-is-cognitive-behavioral-therapy-definition-and-applications.

Oliver, Mary. "The Uses of Sorrow" from Thirst. Boston: Beacon Press, 2007.

Ooms, Vanessa. "Call Your Energy Back." Do It For You, Oct. 29, 2022. https://www.doitforyoubook.com/resources/call-your-energy-back.

Ooms, Vanessa. "Supplemental Material for Do It For You." Do It For You, 2022. http://www.doitforyoubook.com/resources.

Othon, Jack E. "Carl Jung and the Shadow: The Ultimate Guide to the Human Dark Side." High Existence, August 7, 2020. https://www.highexistence.com/carl-jung-shadow-guide-unconscious/.

Pietrangelo, Ann. "The Effects of Stress on Your Body." HealthLine, 2019. https://www.healthline.com/health/stress/effects-on-body.

Raypole, Crystal. "What Are the Signs of Codependency?." PsychCentral, 2021. https://psychcentral.com/lib/symptoms-signs-of-codependency#what-codependency-is.

Robbins, Mel. "The Mistake Everyone Makes with Boundaries." Mel Robbins Facebook Page, April 21, 2022. https://www.facebook.com/watch/?v=1085148852064464.

Russel, Kristin. "Yoga Quotes of B.K.S. Iyengar." July 21, 2015. https://masteringyoga.org/yoga-quotes-of-b-k-s-iyengar-the-body-is-your-temple-keep-it/.

"Scope Creep." Wikipedia, accessed August 15, 2022. https://en.wikipedia.org/wiki/Scope_creep.

"Sanctuary for Your Mind & Soul." Journey. https://journey.cloud/.

Smithsonian Institution,."What Does it Mean to be Human?." Smithsonian National Museum of Natural History, last updated July 7, 2022. https://humanorigins.si.edu/human-characteristics/social-life.

Specktor, Brandon. "How Much Water Do You Really Need to Drink?." Live Science, last updated Oct. 6, 2022. https://www.livescience.com/61353-how-much-water-you-really-need-drink.html.

Steinem, Gloria. *The Truth Will Set You Free, But First It Will Piss You Off!: Thoughts on Life, Love, and Rebellion.* New York: Random House, 2019.

Suzuki, Shunryu. *Zen Mind, Beginner's Mind: Informal Talks on Zen Meditation and Practice.* Colorado: Shambala Publications, Inc., 1970.

The Tapping Solution LLC. "Tapping 101." The Tapping Solution, accessed on August 22, 2022. https://www.thetappingsolution.com/tapping-101/.

"Understanding the Stress Response." Harvard Health Publishing, July 6, 2020. https://www.health.harvard.edu/staying-healthy/understanding-the-stress-response.

"What is EMDR?." EMDR Institute, Inc., accessed on September 16, 2022. https://www.emdr.com/what-is-emdr/.

"What is Quantum Healing Hypnosis Technique?." Dolores Cannon, accessed on August 29, 2022. https://dolorescannon.com/about-qhht/.

Wolynn, Mark. *It Didn't Start with You: How Inherited Family Trauma Shapes Who We Are and How to End the Cycle.* New York: Penguin Books, 2016.

Young, Emma. "Lifting the Lid on the Unconscious." New Scientist, 2018. https://www.newscientist.com/article/mg23931880-400-lifting-the-lid-on-the-unconscious/.

RESOURCES FOR MENTAL & PHYSICAL HEALTH / SAFETY

IF YOU ARE IN DIRE CRISIS

Canadians:
Call the Canada Suicide Prevention Service at 1-833-456-4566 (24/7) or text 45645 (4 pm to 12 am ET)

Americans:
Call 1-800-273-8255 or
visit the Suicide Prevention Lifeline at www.988lifeline.org to chat with someone in real time.

International:
Visit www.findahelpline.com and enter your country to find a crisis line to call and/or a center near you, anywhere in the world!

IF YOU FEEL YOU ARE IN DANGER:

Canada:

ShelterSafe.ca provides information to help connect women and their children across Canada with the nearest shelter for safety and support.

Kids Help Phone
1-800-668-6868
Available to young Canadians between 5 to 29 years old who are seeking 24-hour confidential and anonymous care with professional counselors

Hope for Wellness 24/7 Help Line
1-855-242-3310
Available to all Indigenous peoples across Canada who are seeking immediate crisis intervention.

Childhelp Child Abuse 24/7 Hotline (multilingual):
1-800-422-4453
Help with finding the contact information of the child protection service in your area.

There is a lot more information available at this link:
https://www.canada.ca/en/public-health/services/health-promotion/stop-family-violence/services.html

United States:

The National Domestic Violence Hotline
1-800-799-7233 (SAFE)

www.ndvh.org

National Dating Abuse Helpline
1-866-331-9474

www.loveisrespect.org

National Child Abuse Hotline/Childhelp
1-800-4-A-CHILD (1-800-422-4453)

www.childhelp.org

National Sexual Assault Hotline
1-800-656-4673 (HOPE)

www.rainn.org

International:

https://www.mysticmag.com/psychic-reading/domestic-violence-resource-guide/

Search for your country to find a domestic violence hotline specific to your area.

You are never alone.

ABOUT THE AUTHOR

Vanessa Ooms is an Author, YouTuber, Entrepreneur, Graphic Designer, Meditation Instructor and personal development nut. She's also the founder of Evolving on Purpose™, an online community where people can come together to meet others who are exploring personal development and actively creating better lives for themselves.

Vanessa has been to hell and back… after hitting rock bottom in 2015 and realizing that her addiction to alcohol and overachieving were just band-aids trying to cover a gaping wound in her soul, she decided to find a holistic and healthy way to rebuild her entire life from the ground up. She dove into recovery, constellation therapy, meditation and personal development with a tenacious ferver. Vanessa worked with healers and coaches in a variety of modalities, deepened her spiritual life, read every self-help book she could find, and conducted hundreds of experiments on her mind, body and spirit.

Her mission is to share the holistic wellness practices she's discovered through years of deep shadow work, spiritual exploration, mindset shifts and somatic healing. She wants to help others to heal, fulfill their purpose, feel confident, and remember that they are worthy of all the things that they desire in life.

Her debut book, *Do It For You*, will open up new doors to creating your very best life, offering insights, straight talk and candid commentary about living life…*on purpose.*

LET'S CONNECT!

g Vanessa Ooms

Vanessa Ooms

@vanessaooms

@vanooms

Evolving on Purpose™ with Vanessa Ooms

vanessa@vanessaooms.com

www.vanessaooms.com

Photos by Meredith Rose Photography

If you enjoyed this book, please take a moment to review it on Amazon or GoodReads. Every review is appreciated.

CPSIA information can be obtained
at www.ICGtesting.com
Printed in the USA
BVHW081511040123
655546BV00004B/158